CHECKLIST

FOR A

PERFECT MOVE

Main Street Books
D O U B L E D A Y

New York
London
Toronto
Sydney
Auckland

CHECKLIST

FOR A

PERFECT MOVE

ANNE COLBY

A MAIN STREET BOOK
PUBLISHED BY DOUBLEDAY
a division of Bantam Doubleday Dell Publishing Group, Inc.
1540 Broadway, New York, New York 10036

MAIN STREET BOOKS, DOUBLEDAY, and the portrayal of a building
with a tree are trademarks of Doubleday, a division of
Bantam Doubleday Dell Publishing Group, Inc.

Book design by Claire Naylon Vaccaro

Library of Congress Cataloging-in-Publication Data

Colby, Anne, 1946–
Checklist for a perfect move / by Anne Colby. —1st Main Street
book ed.
p.   cm.
"Main Street books."
1. Moving, Household—United States—Handbooks, manuals, etc.
I. Title.
TX307.C65   1996
648′.9—dc20   95-48101
CIP

ISBN 0-385-47995-6

1   3   5   7   9   10   8   6   4   2

Acknowledgments

I would like to thank my agents Betsy Amster and Angela Miller for making this book happen. I would also like to acknowledge and thank my editors at Doubleday, Rob Robertson and Amy Chapman. They have been most patient and helpful in shepherding this book through the editing process.

On a personal note, my thanks to Laurie, Robert, Margot, P.K., Tom, Dan, Chris, and Dolly. Your assistance has been much appreciated!

Contents

Setting Up the Move   38

Out-of-State Moves   40

Types of Movers . . . How They Charge . . . How to
Find Them . . . Getting an Estimate . . . Binding vs.
Nonbinding Estimates . . . Negotiations . . . Choosing
a Mover . . . Order for Service . . . Changes or
Cancellation . . . Scheduling . . . Protection for Your
Goods . . . Packing . . . Moving Day . . . Inventory
Report . . . Bill of Lading . . . Loading . . . Weighing
Your Shipment . . . Payment . . . Delivery . . . Legal
Protections . . . Filing a Claim . . . Common Moving
Terms

Local Moves   62

How They Charge . . . Getting an Estimate . . . Liability
Protection . . . Choosing a Mover . . . Moving Day

Do-It-Yourself Moves   66

Renting a Truck . . . What They Charge . . . Making
Your Selection . . . How Much Truck Do You Need? . . .
Inventory Checklist . . . Accessories . . . Calculating
Costs . . . Protection . . . Helpers . . . Loading the
Truck . . . Lifting . . . Driving Tips . . . On the
Road . . . Road Emergencies . . . Unloading . . . Towing
Your Car

Children   117

Pets   123

Plants   127

Tax Considerations   129

Corporate Moves   132

Introduction

There's no getting around it. Moving to a new home is *work*. There is the sheer physical effort involved in organizing, packing, transporting, and unpacking your belongings. Then there are all those decisions to make, details to remember, people to contact. And of course there is the emotional adjustment of settling into a new home and community.

And yet moving is exciting, too. It represents a chance for a fresh start. You might be changing cities to accept a new job, or maybe you're finally buying your first home. Perhaps you are moving to a retirement home. No matter what the reason for the move, it will bring new experiences and opportunities.

The average American moves nearly twelve times in the course of a lifetime. I've already hit my quota. On my first moves, in my early twenties, everything I owned fit into, or on top of, my car. But I have also used a small local mover, rented and driven moving vans, leased storage lockers, and called upon friends and family to help me more often than I would like to admit. My favorite move: a corporate relocation where the professional packers and movers did most of the work and the company picked up the tab.

These experiences and my years as a writer on consumer topics have led me to believe that there is one important thing you can do to get good service from a mover: Ask questions.

Wondering if you can get a discount on that truck rental? Ask! Does the mover's liability coverage offer replacement value or only depreciated value for your goods? Ask. Will the company fill out an inventory sheet for a local move? Ask.

Now, more than ever, it is vital that you choose your mover carefully. In 1996, Congress abolished the Interstate Commerce Commission, which regulated the household-goods moving industry. Some of ICC's responsibilities, such as licensing, were transferred to the Federal Highway Administration's Office of Motor Carriers. But while industry regulations still exist, FHWA at this writing had no funds to enforce them.

While researching this book, I called moving companies and posed as a consumer planning a move. By asking key questions, I was able to uncover important information that would have swayed my choice of mover had I really been considering a move. None of the companies volunteered this information. I had to ask. You should do the same.

The second thing to remember is that you should always call around and get bids from several different companies. Compare prices, services, and attitudes and negotiate to get the best deal. This is a highly competitive industry. Use that to your advantage.

This book gives you a big head start. It explains the moving process and tells you exactly what you need to do at each step along the way. It points out the questions you should ask. Whether you're eagerly anticipating the move, or just doing it out of necessity, this book can help make it a more manageable and pleasant experience.

- The first section of the book offers a detailed timeline for everything that needs to get done in the weeks before the move. Use this as your master "to do" list and check off items as you complete them. It will save you from such minor disasters as forgetting to rent the moving van, mail your change-of-address cards, or make your travel reservations.

- The sections on out-of-state and local moves explain how moving companies work and show you how to protect yourself from shoddy operators. You'll also learn how to negotiate the best deals and get the most reliable service from your mover.

- A budget move can be just as well-organized as one using professional movers. Do-it-yourself movers and those packing their own belongings will find a complete step-by-step guide to doing it right. You'll learn how to choose the appropriate size of truck and packing materials for your household. You'll also get packing tips from the professionals.

- You'll find ideas on helping children adjust to the move and suggestions for keeping them involved. Pets and plants also require special considerations—you'll learn what they are.

- On the business side of things, there are guides to deducting moving expenses from your taxes, negotiating a company-financed move, and filing a claim against a moving company for damaged goods.

It's time to jump in and get to work. Your adventure is about to begin! Take a deep breath and read on. Best wishes for a successful move.

CHECKLIST

FOR A

PERFECT MOVE

Four to Six Weeks
Before the Move

S o much to do in the next several weeks!
You can greatly reduce the stress of moving by
doing a little bit each week, rather than all at once
in the last few days. Write your change-of-address cards on
one night; go through a closet on another. Spreading the
tasks out over the course of several weeks will help you feel
calmer and more in control. Your family will feel the difference and the move will go smoother.

Use this timeline to keep yourself on track. It covers
all the details of the move, whether you're making a major
relocation across the country or just moving to a nicer
neighborhood on the other side of town. Check off the
items as you complete them and ignore those that do not
apply to your situation.

Although it will seem like the list of things to do
never ends, be sure to set aside time each day to relax, have
fun, and share the excitement of moving. Look at the next
several weeks as a time not only to complete necessary
chores but to plan for a new future. At the end of each
day, take a few minutes to meditate, luxuriate in a hot
bath, or relax with a cup of tea or glass of wine. Renew
your energy before the next day begins.

Moving Arrangements

◉   Put together a calendar showing the weeks leading up to your move. Post it where everyone can see, on the family bulletin board or the refrigerator. Jot down estimate appointments, garage sale dates, going-away celebrations, possible moving days.

◉   If an employer is paying for some or all of your moving expenses, find out exactly what expenses it will be covering. What kinds of documentation does it need and what forms do you need to fill out? How will the company be handling payment?

◉   Contact your accountant or the Internal Revenue Service for the latest information on tax-deductible expenses. Start a folder to keep track of expenses and receipts.

◉   Ask friends, neighbors, and relatives to recommend moving companies they have used and liked. Go through the Yellow Pages for additional companies. Call up the movers and interview them about their services. Choose three that sound the best and schedule times to have their representatives come to your home to give estimates.

◉   Before the estimators arrive, think about what extra services you might want. Do you want packing and unpacking? Storage-in-transit? Are there special circumstances, such as stairs or elevators on the other end, that will affect the price? Do you want them to move your car? Give each mover the same information so you are comparing apples with apples. Be sure to ask about liability coverage for your belongings. Tell them you are comparison shopping and ask for a discount.

◉   If you think you might want to ship some of your

goods, call freight companies and the postal service for current rates.

◎   Call auto transporters to compare prices for getting your car to your new home.

◎   Putting some boxes or furniture into permanent storage? Call around for estimates and visit the facilities.

◎   If you plan to rent a truck to move your own things, call around for estimates. Ask about prices for dollies, pads, and other accessories. Make your reservations well in advance.

◎   Talk with your insurance agent about coverage for your household goods while they are in transit. Compare prices with the liability coverage the moving company offers. If you are transporting valuables, ask about adding a floater to the policy. Ask about coverage for you and your helpers.

◎   Select a moving company and reserve dates for the move.

◎   If you are traveling to your destination by air, train, or bus, start shopping around for the best deal.

◎   Inquire about fares, restrictions, and requirements for transporting your pet if you have one. Make an appointment with your veterinarian to arrange immunization shots if necessary, order a new identification tag, and get copies of health records.

Moving Services Checklist

Before you get estimates from potential movers, you should have an idea of what services you want. Go through the house and evaluate your belongings. What items do you plan to take? Any oversized pieces? Will any aspect of the move be physically challenging? What services might you want movers to provide? What level of liability protection do you want? What dates are best for the move? Fill out this checklist and use it as a guide in your meetings with movers.

LARGE ITEMS TO BE MOVED

Refrigerator	_____	Oversized table	_____
Freezer	_____	Office desk	_____
Washer	_____	Sofa bed	_____
Dryer	_____	Reclining chair	_____
Dishwasher	_____	Playhouse or shed	_____
Oversized couch	_____	Spa or whirlpool	_____
Entertainment unit	_____	Car or motorcycle	_____
Big-screen TV	_____	Boat	_____
Piano or keyboard	_____	Camper/trailer	_____
Pool table	_____	Riding-style mower	_____
Grandfather clock	_____	Snowmobile	_____
Large armoire	_____	Other	_____

VALUABLE ITEMS TO BE CRATED

China	_____
Crystal	_____
Ceramics	_____
Antique furniture	_____
Chandelier	_____
Fine art	_____
Other	_____

SPECIAL SERVICES

Packing	_____	Furniture	
Crating	_____	breakdown	_____
Appliance servicing	_____	Storage-in-transit	_____

Unpacking	_____	Space reservation	_____
Vehicle transport	_____	Truck reservation	_____
Specific pickup day	_____	Relocation services	_____
Specific delivery day	_____	Other	_____

SPECIAL CIRCUMSTANCES—PICKUP

Elevator _____
Stairs _____
Long carry to curb _____
Tight corners _____
Small doorways _____
Parking problems _____
More than one
   pickup _____
Other _____

SPECIAL CIRCUMSTANCES—DELIVERY

Elevator _____
Stairs _____
Long carry to curb _____
Tight corners _____
Small doorways _____
Parking problems _____
Additional location _____
Other _____

MOVING DATES

PACKING DAY
First choice _____
Second choice _____
Third choice _____

Not before   _____
Not on   _____
Not after   _____

MOVING DAY
First choice   _____
Second choice   _____
Third choice   _____
Not before   _____
Not on   _____
Not after   _____

DELIVERY DAY
First choice   _____
Second choice   _____
Third choice   _____
Not before   _____
Not on   _____
Not after   _____

LIABILITY COVERAGE

.60 lb. (free)   _____
Depreciated value   _____
Replacement value   _____
R.V. w/ deductible _____
Other   _____

Cleaning and Organizing

◎ Begin going through every room of the house and
evaluating your possessions. Don't forget the closets,
attic, basement, garage, and storage areas. What can be

sold or given away? What can be packed up early? Will any of your belongings need special treatment in the move? Organize drawers, closets, and storage areas to make them easier to pack. Go through the house and get rid of things you don't need.

- Take a room-by-room inventory of everything you own, using the Inventory Checklist on pages 70–74 as a guide. Photograph or videotape your possessions for insurance purposes. List items of value, including electronics equipment, collectibles, furnishings, silver, and china. Put receipts into one file or estimate purchase price and year of purchase of each item. Contact a professional appraiser to document the worth of antiques and exceptionally valuable items.

- Draw a to-scale floor plan of your new home. Make paper cutouts of your furniture and try out different room arrangements. Do a final floor plan for each room. This process will make move-in day easier and help you decide what you don't need.

- Have a garage sale to get rid of things you don't want to move. Donate the rest to charity and keep the receipts for tax purposes.

- Do any repair work and painting needed on your current residence.

- Start using up foods you have on hand, especially frozen, perishable, and canned goods. Buy only food items you absolutely need from now on.

Packing

- If you are doing your own packing, start collecting or buying boxes and other moving materials, including unprinted newspaper, marking pens, and plastic tape. Put aside old blankets, rope, and newspapers.

◉ Begin packing seldom-used articles. If you're moving during the summer, pack heavy blankets and holiday supplies. In the winter, your camping supplies and sports equipment can be packed early. Be careful not to pack something you might need before or during the move.

◉ Collect and keep important documents and records handy. Keep them with you when you travel; do not send them with movers.

Transferring Records

◉ Contact your doctors, dentist, pharmacist, veterinarian, attorney, and real estate agent to notify them of your move and ask for referrals. Arrange for records to be transferred or sent to you. Transfer prescriptions with your doctor's help.

◉ Contact your insurance agents and ask how you can transfer your insurance (home, auto, boat) so protection is continuous.

◉ Notify your children's schools about the move and give them your new address for the forwarding of your children's transcripts and other documents. Ask teachers to provide recommendations if appropriate.

◉ Contact your banking institutions to find out what you need to do to transfer funds to a bank in your new city or state.

◉ Close out local charge accounts you don't need.

◉ Clear outstanding tax assessments and bills.

Notifying People

◉ If you are a renter, give written notice to your landlord according to the terms specified in your lease. Find out the requirements for getting your deposit back and when you can expect it. Give the landlord your new address.

◉ If you own your home, talk to your real estate agent about the move. If you haven't yet sold your house, ask the broker to put extra energy into getting potential buyers into the home while it is still occupied. Work out the logistics for transferring keys and documents to the real estate agent or new buyer.

◉ Make a list of everyone you need to notify about your move, including businesses, utilities, and personal friends. Use the Address Change Checklist on page 10 as a guide.

◉ Send the post office a change-of-address form thirty days in advance of the move or as soon as you can. One postcard for your whole family will be enough.

The post office will forward your first-class mail for one year at no charge, but there will be at least a three- to five-day delay in receiving it. Magazines, newspapers, and other periodicals—second-class mail—will be forwarded for sixty days for no charge. Circulars, books, catalogs, and advertising mail weighing less than 16 ounces are classified as third-class mail and will not be forwarded unless the mailer requests it. Fourth-class parcel post packages weighing 16 ounces or more will be forwarded locally at no charge for one year; you pay forwarding charges if you move outside the area.

◉ Call friends and relatives to let them know when and where you're moving. Invite them to a going-away party by phone or written invitation.

◉ To save time, fill out one change-of-address card with your new address, then take it with a package of four- inch by five-inch blank unlined index cards to a quick- print shop to have duplicates made.

◉   Tape your old mailing label on magazine change-of-address cards to help publishers locate your account.

◉   When you receive monthly bills, note your new address on them when sending in your payment. Always include the apartment number.

◉   Notify organizations and ask to have memberships transferred when this is possible. You may be able to get partial refunds on memberships in local clubs and organizations if you are leaving the area.

◉   Ask your church or temple for a referral in your new area. Arrange for an introduction or letter of recommendation.

◉   Check your daily mail to see if you've forgotten anyone who should have your new address. Keep records of those you have notified.

Address Change Checklist

_____ Accountant
_____ Alumni associations
_____ Attorneys
_____ Banks
_____ Book or music clubs
_____ Catalog merchants
_____ Charities
_____ Church/synagogue
_____ Club memberships
_____ Credit cards
_____ Credit unions
_____ Dentist
_____ Department stores
_____ Employers
_____ Frequent flyer
        programs
_____ Friends and relatives
_____ Government benefits
_____ Insurance
        companies
_____ Investment
        companies
_____ IRS and state tax
        agencies
_____ Magazines and
        journals
_____ Motor vehicle
        department
_____ Newspapers
_____ Pharmacist
_____ Physicians

_____ Post offices, old and   _____ Union
        new   _____ Veterans
_____ Savings and loan   administration
_____ Social security   _____ Veterinarian
_____ Stockbroker   _____ Voter registration

Family Matters

◉ Talk to your children about the move if you haven't yet done so. Explain all of the advantages to them and listen to their concerns and fears. Discuss what you all can do to make the move a positive experience for everyone.

◉ Make each family member a part of the planning process. Help them put together a calendar of activities leading up to the move. Come to an agreement about what their pre-move responsibilities will be, what they will pack, and what they will do on packing day, the day of the move, and the day you arrive.

◉ On a bulletin board or the refrigerator door put together a family communication center for notes, questions, and a move calendar.

Getting Your New Home Ready

It helps to start the settling-in process well before you get to your new home. You will want to make sure the house is in move-in condition, contact service providers you will need right away, and get your children registered in school. Start tackling these chores now and spread them out throughout the next month or so as time and necessity dictate.

◉ Order business and residential telephone directories for your new community. Subscribe to the local newspaper while still in your old home. This way you can familiarize yourself with local services, news, and community activities.

- Ask the former owners of your new house for referrals to contractors and other service providers. Ask them to leave warranties and service manuals for furnace and appliances.

- Contact painters, carpenters, plumbers, roofers to work on your new home so it is ready when you arrive. Arrange for a locksmith to change the locks on the doors after the home becomes vacant.

- Look into a home security system for the house.

- Set up lawn care and gardening services.

- Arrange other ongoing services you will need right away, such as child care.

- Arrange start dates for utilities and basic services in your new home. Find out what is needed to get deposits transferred or waived. Ask which day the trash is collected and whether there is a recycling program.

- Compare local banking services and choose a new bank, or arrange to transfer holdings from your current bank to your new one. Set up an account in your new destination before you arrive so you don't have to cash out-of-state checks.

- Check school schedules and enrollment requirements. Select new schools for your children. Start the process of transferring school records as soon as possible.

- Locate doctors and other professionals.

- Contact the local chamber of commerce for information on shopping, dining, and services in your new area. Many movers also provide this information.

- Contact city hall or your auto club for a local map, voter registration forms, and pet registration information.

- ◎ Call the state department of motor vehicles for information on changing your driver's license and auto registration. If you are moving to a new state, write or call to find out how to apply for a license and how much of a grace period you are allowed. If you are moving out of the United States, ask the consulate or your moving consultant about how to obtain an international driver's license.
- ◎ If you want to join a club or need to get a license or permit at your new location, apply now. Join a health club or transfer an existing membership.
- ◎ Contact your town's department of parks and recreation for information on playgrounds and recreational activities. Inquire about Little League, scout troops, and classes for your children.
- ◎ Locate the hospital, police, and fire stations near your new home. Make up a list of emergency and important phone numbers (see the Important Numbers checklist on pages 143–44).
- ◎ Scout your new neighborhood to find the best stores for groceries, furniture, and supplies you will need right away.

Two Weeks Before
the Move

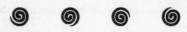

Moving Arrangements

- Confirm dates and arrangements with your moving company. If you've sold, given away, or acquired items since the moving company made its bid, ask if the original estimate still covers everything. The company may need to issue a change order.
- Plan your trip in detail. Map your route if you are driving. Reserve overnight accommodations. Make any last reservations, including those for your pet. Put tickets, confirmations, itinerary, and maps in a special file.
- Make arrangements to have cars, boats, or trailers shipped if you haven't yet done so.
- If you are moving yourself, confirm your reservation with the truck rental agency or make a reservation if you haven't yet done so. Finalize arrangements with those who will be helping you pack and move.
- Contact your building manager to schedule use of the elevators.
- Service your car, especially if traveling a long distance. A complete tune-up is a good idea. Be sure to have brakes, tires, oil, water, fan belt, and windshield wipers

checked. Check your antifreeze if you're moving from a warm to a cold climate. Clean out the car's interior.

◎ Arrange for a baby-sitter and pet boarding for packing day and the day of the move. If you don't know the exact day yet, make contingencies for each day in the spread.

Cleaning and Organizing

◎ If you are putting your household items in storage, you may find it helpful to take photographs of your furniture, bedspread, lamps, and area carpets to use as a reference when you are shopping for drapes, carpeting, or paint for your new home.

◎ Make a list of everything inside your refrigerator and cupboards to use as your master shopping list in stocking your new home's pantry.

◎ Have rugs and carpets cleaned. Measure rugs before you send them out and ask the cleaner to wrap them. If this is a local move, have rugs delivered to the new house after you move in. If not, when you get them back, write the dimensions and rug location on the outside wrapping and keep them packaged for the move. Wait until after you move to send draperies and curtains to the cleaner.

◎ Clean the oven and refrigerator, as well as kitchen shelves and drawers, so that on packing day you'll only have to wipe them out.

◎ Throw away anything that may leak or is explosive or flammable, such as spray paints, solvents, and thinners.

◎ Go through the medicine cabinet and throw away outdated medications. Seal the rest with masking tape if need be. Refill prescriptions before you leave.

◎ Return any items your family has on loan, such as
   library books. Retrieve items other people have borrowed from you.
◎ Get seasonal items out of storage.
◎ Arrange for pre- and post-move appliance servicing
   with a repair person or through your moving company.
   Also arrange to have grandfather clocks, pool tables,
   chandeliers, television antennas, and any other special
   items readied for shipment.
◎ Give away plants or prepare them for the trip in your
   car (see the Plants section on pages 127–28).

Packing

◎ If you are moving yourself or shipping some of your
   goods separately, obtain all necessary packing materials.
   Begin packing those items you won't need over the next
   two weeks. Be sure to label everything well. Designate a
   couple of empty closets or a little-used room as temporary holding places.
◎ Pack boxes that you plan to ship through the post
   office or other delivery service.
◎ If you are driving, pack up the car emergency kit.

Transferring Records

◎ Arrange disconnect dates with the local utilities, including garbage, water, telephone, gas, oil, electric,
   long-distance service, and cable companies. Give yourself an extra day or two of service after your departure
   date just in case there is an unforeseen delay. Ask for a
   refund of your deposits and letters of referral from your
   utility companies to avoid paying deposits at your new

home. Set up utilities in your new home, with start
dates of one to two days before you are due to arrive.

- If you haven't yet done so, terminate other services,
such as gardener, pool maintenance, and housekeeping.
Arrange for these services at your new home.

- Make arrangements with your home security company to stop service or continue it until the new owners
take possession of the house.

Stop/Start Service

	Company	Phone
Cable TV		
Old		
New		
Diaper service		
Old		
New		
Electric		
Old		
New		
Fuel		
Old		
New		
Gas		
Old		
New		
Garbage		
Old		
New		
Gardening		
Old		
New		
Home security		
Old		
New		

Contact	Date Called	Stop/Start Date

	Company	Phone
Housecleaning		
Old		
New		
Laundry		
Old		
New		
Newspaper		
Old		
New		
Pool service		
Old		
New		
Telephone		
Old		
New		
Long-distance		
Old		
New		
Water		
Old		
New		
Other		
Old		
New		

Contact	Date Called	Stop/Start Date

Staying in Touch

◉ Mail any remaining change-of-address cards.

◉ Take care of your good-bye phone calls early, so you aren't doing it all in the last few days when you will be busy with the move. Ask friends, neighbors, and relatives to pick up items you are giving away. Make sure you have everyone's current address and phone number in your address book.

Family Matters

◉ Schedule a few short family meetings in these last weeks to solve problems, offer reassurances, discuss activity schedules, assign moving tasks, and gauge feelings about the move.

Loose Ends

◉ If your old home has not been sold yet, hire someone to mow the lawn, shovel snow, and take out the garbage after you go. Borrow or buy some old lamps to put on timers after you move out to give the appearance that the house is still occupied and prevent vandalism.

One Week Before the Move

@ @ @ @

Moving Arrangements

- Confirm arrival time and final details with the moving company or truck rental agency. Write out the directions to your new home to give to the driver on the day of the move. Include the phone numbers of the places you are staying en route and your new home, your new employer's phone number, and alternate contact numbers.

- Obtain cash or a certified or cashier's check to pay the driver, unless your employer is paying for your move. If you have a nonbinding estimate, buy traveler's checks to cover the 10 percent extra you must pay if the price exceeds the estimate by that much or more.

- If your employer is paying for the move, check to make sure the mover has received a purchase order or letter of authority. Make sure your company doesn't think they are to reimburse *you*.

- Drop off boxes to be shipped by the post office, packaging or express service, or other shipper.

- Arrange for transportation to the airport if you are flying.

◎   Call to confirm packing and moving dates with your children's and pet's sitters.

Cleaning and Organizing

◎   Take a final inventory, noting any current damage to your belongings. Check your home for remaining items you may want to discard.

◎   Remove breakables, spillables, and small items like jewelry from drawers.

◎   Locate original cartons and manuals for your electronic equipment so that it can be packed according to the manufacturer's specifications.

◎   Do your last laundry before the trip.

◎   Empty and clean garbage cans you will be taking with you. Drain your garden hoses.

◎   Drain fuel and oil from the lawn mower, snowblower, and other power equipment. Empty the barbecue tank, clean the grill, and pack loose parts.

◎   Take down draperies, drapery rods, and attachable shelving moving with you.

◎   Finish minor repair work.

◎   Disconnect and prepare your major appliances for the move. Disconnect and cap the gas line to a clothes dryer and secure the tub of a clothes washer.

◎   Use up, give away, or throw out food you're not taking with you.

◎   Dispose of any houseplants that you're not taking.

◎   Clean your new home and make any needed repairs if you can. If you plan to paint or wallpaper, try to do it before you move in.

Packing

◎   If you are doing your own packing, spread the task out through the week. Stack boxes in corners so rooms can still be used. Label everything carefully.

◎   Pack or set aside those items that you want to have with you as soon as you arrive at your new home, such as children's items, medicines, and cleaning and kitchen supplies for your first couple of days there. Label these LOAD LAST. Refer to checklists in this book for suggestions.

◎   Set aside soap, toilet paper, paper towels, and cleaning supplies for moving day.

◎   Gather all the documents you will be taking with you and put these in a safe place where they will not be accidentally loaded in the van. Besides your personal and business records, include:

  • van line shipping papers
  • origin and destination agents' telephone numbers
  • emergency telephone numbers of relatives and friends
  • telephone number of truck rental company if you are moving yourself
  • travel documents, including plane or train tickets, reservation confirmations
  • map of your new city

◎   Pack travel suitcases for each family member, including clothing, toiletries, toys, games, and books—enough to meet your needs while your belongings are in transit. If your children are staying with someone else during packing and moving, pack a separate bag for those days.

◎   Pack other items you're taking with you in the car and label DO NOT LOAD. Set these aside in a safe place or in the car trunk. Let children load their personal boxes and day packs for the trip so they feel secure about these items. Put your emergency tool box in the trunk (or load it in the rental van later).

◎ Mark any items that should go to storage.

◎ If you are moving to a temporary residence until your new home is ready, pack items you and your family will need there and set aside. Label these so movers will know where they go.

Transferring Records

◎ Close your bank account or have your current bank transfer funds to your new bank. Keep enough money to tide you over until you are settled into your new home. Include enough for a modest tip for movers at both ends. Withdraw the contents of your safety deposit box. Send these by registered mail to your new post office or consult your mover for names of companies that specialize in transporting valuables.

Staying in Touch

◎ If time permits, give a going-away party. Keep it simple. Use disposable products for easy cleanup.

Family Matters

◎ Help children with their packing chores. Make sure they've collected phone numbers and addresses of friends and said their good-byes.

Loose Ends

◉   Pay any outstanding fines and settle bills with local merchants.

◉   Return rented videotapes; pick up dry cleaning and carpets.

◉   Cancel newspaper delivery.

◉   Buy some prepared foods, snacks, fruit, and drinks for the day of the move. Have hot and cold drinks on hand for packers and movers.

◉   Put together a "hospitality sheet" for the new owners of your home, with names of neighbors, repair people and local services, garden instructions, baby-sitter names, and a city map. Include any other information about the house or the neighborhood that you feel is important to know. Leave this out with furnace directions and appliance manuals and warranties.

One Day
Before the Move

§ § § §

Family Matters

◉ Drop off children and pets at their sitters or have them picked up.

Cleaning and Organizing

◉ Make breakfast and wash all the dishes so they can be packed. Make this your last meal in the house. Clean up the kitchen after your meal. Empty, defrost, if necessary, and dry out your refrigerator/freezer. Place baking soda in each compartment. Block doors open so they can't accidentally close on pets or children. Put soft drinks and lunch foods in a cooler.

◉ Disconnect the TV and other electronics equipment.

◉ Check the gas and oil in your car.

◉ Make sure you have tickets, charge cards, and other essentials for the trip.

Packing

◎ If you are doing your own packing, finish the rest of it today.

◎ Professional packers usually pack on this day. If the packers are late, call your moving company to be sure they're on their way.

◎ Introduce yourself to the packers and walk through the house with them when they arrive. Explain how you have organized rooms and point out items that are fragile. Bring to their attention those items that should not be packed (these should be marked) and those marked DO NOT UNPACK or STORAGE. Ask them to take note of items that should be put in boxes labeled LOAD LAST (cleaning supplies, children's things) because you want easy access to them at your new home. These should also be marked so it is clear to them what goes where.

◎ Keep an eye on packers, but don't get in their way. Treat them with respect and courtesy. If they seem careless or unprofessional, call the moving company. If you hired them independently, make your complaint in a businesslike way and insist that the job be done properly.

◎ Inspect boxes when the packers are finished to be sure they are adequately labeled. Before you sign the manifest, check it thoroughly. Verify the number of boxes packed and that all services have been performed.

◎ Label any other boxes you want loaded last or not loaded at all and make sure these are clearly out of the way of movers.

◎ If you like, tip the packers $10 to $20 for a job well done.

Moving Day

@ @ @ @

Family Matters

◎ Drop children off or have their sitters pick them up early in the day. Make sure older children who are out playing in the neighborhood know what time you expect them home and what time you plan to leave. Check in with children during the day to answer questions, offer emotional support, and give them reassurance.

Cleaning and Organizing

◎ Strip beds. Roll up all the linens, blankets, and pillows and put in boxes marked LOAD LAST, with the name of the person whose bed they belong to, i.e., LINENS: KATE'S BED. You will want access to these right away when you get to the new house.

◎ Put all your important lists on a clipboard.

◎ Put your keys, moving documents, contact phone number, and other important papers in a safe place where they will not get misplaced.

◎ Just before you leave, pack the car with suitcases, travel kits, anything you will be taking with you. Lock

your car and park it in a secure garage or a very safe
spot. Do not leave valuables within view.

◎   Remember to eat properly and drink enough water.
Be careful of your back and general health today.

Do-It-Yourself Moves

◎   If you are moving yourself, pick up the rental truck
and take it for a practice drive. Refer to the Do-It-
Yourself Moves section on pages 66–82 for directions on
loading the truck.

Working with Professional Movers

◎   Keep track of the time movers are due to arrive and
call if they are late.

◎   Be at home when the movers arrive. If you can't be
there, make sure your agent has in writing the name and
telephone number of the person you've authorized to
take your place. It's best if two adults can be present—
one to oversee the move process, the other to clean
rooms as they are emptied.

◎   Tour your home with the driver or van foreman to
examine the goods to be moved and what should not be
moved. Establish a friendly rapport. Discuss travel and
arrival times to make sure your plans are in agreement.
Accompany the foreman as he inspects and tags each
piece of furniture with an identifying number and
records the condition of each piece on the inventory
sheet. Indicate which boxes should be loaded last so
they can be unloaded first at the new house.

◎   Check that your new address and phone number are
correct on the bill of lading, which is your receipt. Read
this and the inventory sheet carefully to make sure you

agree with the foreman's comments before you sign them. If you notice any damage to the residence, note this on your copy of the inventory and the foreman's copy.

◎ Add the bill of lading and inventory sheet to your other moving documents and keep everything in a safe place until all charges have been paid and any claims have been settled.

◎ Check the conditions of items as they're loaded.

◎ Sweep and dust rooms after everything is moved out of them.

◎ After loading and before the movers have left, tour your home again to make sure nothing is forgotten. Look through closets, permanent drawers, cubbyholes, attic, basement, garage, storage areas.

◎ Tipping is not expected, but a moderate tip of $10 apiece for movers and $20 for the foreman will convey your appreciation for good work.

Closing Up the House

◎ Check all built-in appliances, heating, and air conditioning to make sure everything is turned off. Take out the trash.

◎ Leave your "hospitality sheet" on a kitchen counter for the new owners. Be sure to leave your new address and phone number so they can forward mail.

◎ Turn off the lights; close and lock all the windows and doors. Time to say good-bye to your old home!

◎ Leave the residence only after the moving truck is gone.

◎ Drop the house keys off with the real estate agent, landlord, or another trusted person.

Getting to Your New Home

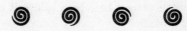

- ◎ Have your truck rental company phone number handy in case of road emergency if you are moving yourself.
- ◎ If movers are transporting your things, keep your moving documents file handy.
- ◎ Keep a log of mileage and receipts for everything—gasoline, tolls, parking, hotels, fares. Meals are not tax-deductible, but if your employer is paying for the move they will probably be covered.
- ◎ Make the trip fun. Play games with the kids, tell stories, sing songs. Talk with them about the things they can do in their new home, friends they will meet, trips you can take in a new city. Make your move a minivacation.

    Don't drive all night or rush to your new home. Get enough sleep so you are rested for the busy days ahead.

Delivery Day

@ @ @ @

Before the Movers Arrive

@ If you're moving a long distance, call the moving company's local agent as soon as you arrive in your new city to inquire about when the van is scheduled to arrive. Tell him where you can be reached and make final arrangements to receive your goods.

@ Check the house completely. Test the plumbing, heating and air conditioning, electrical outlets, built-in appliances, and smoke detectors. Arrange for appliance installation.

@ Start cleaning the house if needed. Paper shelves and prepare closets. Do minor repair work, painting, and wallpapering.

@ Post floor plans in every room so movers know how the furniture should be arranged. Make signs for every room indicating its purpose, i.e., den, office, or baby's nursery.

Family Matters

◎ Take a few minutes to tour the house with your children. Talk to them about what will happen over the next two days and what you expect of them.

◎ Have some toys or games on hand for kids to play with while you are busy with the house. Or give them an unpacking or cleanup project. Children may enjoy setting up their new bedrooms, playing in the yard, or exploring the new neighborhood. Make sure they know their boundaries and what time they should return. If they need supervision, trade off with your partner or arrange for extra help.

Do-It-Yourself Moves

◎ Set up the loading ramp.

◎ Post room-by-room floor plans with furniture diagrams so helpers know where to put things.

◎ Unload everything from the truck. Put each item in the room in which it belongs so you don't have to move it twice.

◎ When you're done unloading, inspect the truck, front and back, to check for items you might have missed.

◎ Lock up the house and return the truck or leave one person behind to start unpacking.

Working with Professional Movers

◎ Be at your new home when the driver arrives.

◎ Pay the driver or foreman with cash, money order, certified check, or traveler's check. Movers are required to collect payment before unloading anything. They usually can't take a personal check.

◎ Ideally, two people should be available to direct the movers. One person stands by the truck with a copy of the inventory and checks for damage. The second person stands at the front door and directs the movers.

◎ Use your floor plan to assist the driver with proper furniture placement. Ask that boxes labeled UNLOAD FIRST be placed where they are easily accessed. Check to see that every box is in the right room and furniture is correctly placed before movers leave. They should reassemble standard items, such as beds that they took apart to move.

◎ You may not want to have movers unpack all the boxes. It's disorienting to have everything strewn all over the house. You can unpack and check the condition of items over the next few days. However, you may want movers to unpack large items, such as mattresses, wardrobes, lamps, and mirrors. Make arrangements for this when you are negotiating the terms of the move.

◎ Take a careful inventory of your household goods and look for damage. Open and inspect any boxes that look damaged. Check your inventory sheets. List any problems you find and make a note that you have not yet approved the condition of all your possessions.

◎ Do not sign the inventory sheet until you have checked off all inventory numbers and made notes regarding visible damage. The company will need to refer to these sheets if you file a claim.

◎ Tip the movers if you are happy with their work.

Setting Up the House

◎ If it is very cold outside, allow televisions and appliances to warm up to room temperature before using them.

- ◎ Unpack the boxes you marked LOAD LAST. These should contain bedding, kitchen supplies, cleaning materials, children's things, and other things you will need today. (See checklists for items to include in these boxes.)

- ◎ Arrange children's rooms first. Put furniture in place and make the beds. Push boxes into corners and clear the room of clutter. Plug in a lamp and turn back the beds to create a comforting environment for the kids. If they're old enough, let kids unpack and decorate themselves.

- ◎ Unpack the kitchen next. Don't worry about arranging everything exactly as it's going to be forever. Instead concentrate on getting it ready for your immediate use. Stock the kitchen with items you'll need in order to prepare meals over the next few days. Put away dishes, glassware, utensils.

- ◎ Unpack your own bedroom, make the bed, and set up a couple of lamps. Unpack and put away clothes, shoes, cosmetics, and toiletries you will use over the next day or two.

- ◎ Set up the laundry. You'll need it soon.

- ◎ Unpack the living room, dining room, and other common areas.

- ◎ Flatten boxes and store them in an out-of-the-way place for the next time you move.

- ◎ Do as much as you can on the first day, but don't exhaust yourself or your family.

- ◎ Take a dinner break when everyone's hungry. Stop at the supermarket to pick up groceries and cleaning supplies for the next day or two. Have duplicate keys made. Get a good night's sleep.

Setting Up the Move

◉ ◉ ◉ ◉

Your first task is to decide how you will pack and transport your possessions.

◉ Do you want to hire an interstate moving company or a local independent mover?

◉ Do you want to pack and unpack your own things or have the movers do it for you?

◉ Perhaps you want to save money and move everything yourself. In that case, do you need to rent a vehicle or do you own or have access to a truck large enough for your things?

◉ Have you considered shipping some or all of your goods by mail, packaging or express service, air, train, bus, or boat?

These decisions will be based on your budget, time, household size, distance you are moving, and your physical capabilities. The following sections explain all of your options and what methods of moving are best for different situations.

As soon as you know you'll be moving, start calling

around to get information from moving companies and services. If you plan to use a professional mover, six to eight weeks in advance is not too early to start setting up your move. This is especially true if you're moving during the peak season of May to October, on a weekend, or around the first of the month.

Out-of-State Moves

@ @ @ @

I f you're moving out of the state, you'll need to use a
company licensed by the Federal Highway Administration (formerly the Interstate Commerce Commission)
to cross state lines. The good news for consumers is that
interstate movers have to abide by rules and regulations
designed to protect you, your belongings, and your wallet.
But it's still important for you to do your homework when
choosing a moving company. You may find great variance
in price, service, and reliability among different movers.

Types of Movers

@ National van lines are the well-advertised names you
probably already know. A van line is really a network of
agents that operates under the parent company name.
Your load will be handled by several agents as it makes
its way across the country.

To set up the move, you call the "booking agent"
near your current home. The booking agent oversees all
pre-move services, including estimates, packing, and
loading. This agent also registers the move with the par-

ent company, which assigns it to an interstate van going in the direction of your new home. The van may be owned and operated by a company driver, who is also called the "hauling agent." Typically, your shipment is one of several the driver is transporting on that trip.

When your possessions arrive at their destination, the company's agent in that area takes over the management of the job. The "destination agent" coordinates the delivery and assigns workers to help the driver unload and unpack. If you have any claims for damages, you make them through this office.

In addition to transporting your household, some of these movers also offer information about your new community.

◎   You can arrange interstate moves through an independent or family-run company. Typically, these companies perform local, statewide, or regional moves themselves. When arranging interstate moves, they handle the details at the starting point and then link up with an independent mover in your destination city to complete the move. They contract with a driver who typically owns the van that is transporting your goods. In essence, you are working with two separate companies and a driver.

◎   For a budget move, there are movers that provide only the most basic of services: van and driver. The company delivers the van to your house and you do all the packing and loading yourself. The mover then drives your goods across the country. When the van gets to your new home, you do the unloading and unpacking there as well. Depending on your destination, this option can be cheaper than renting a truck and doing the driving yourself.

How They Charge

Interstate moving companies base their charges on the weight of your household goods and the distance they have to travel. They charge extra for stairs, elevators, packing and unpacking, servicing appliances, and moving certain items, such as pianos and cars.

A moving company representative will come to your home to survey your belongings and estimate their weight. They will question you about what services you want and the details of your move. They will then give you a written estimate of the price they will charge to move your household.

You should try to negotiate. Companies operate under a published rate schedule, but are allowed by law to offer discounts. You should always ask for a discount and negotiate the fee. Most movers will offer discounts of up to 50 percent to get your business. You will be able to get the best discounts when your move is an easy one and if you can schedule it in off-peak periods, such as in November to April, in midweek, and on days other than the first and last of the month.

If you have only a few things to move, you should be aware that some carriers may have minimum charges. The carrier may have a minimum weight of 5,000 pounds, So even if the total weight of your shipment is 3,000 pounds, you will still pay for 5,000 pounds. If your household is small, you might be better off shipping your goods by another method and selling those heavy items you can replace for less than it costs to move them.

How to Find Them

How do you find a good carrier? As with any service, start by asking people you know for their recommendations. They will probably have strong opinions about movers they have used. Your real estate agent may be able to offer recommendations based on the experiences of clients. Neighbors, friends, relatives, coworkers—all may be able to offer leads.

- Look through the business pages of your local telephone directory to see the range of moving companies available. Display ads will give you an idea of each company's particular specialty. Call a number of them to compare their services and see how they sound over the phone.

- You can get names of companies from mover associations, the chamber of commerce, local business groups, and consumer organizations. Ask if they know of any companies that have been in business a long time and are well-respected in the industry.

- Once you have collected names, addresses, business license numbers, and phone numbers of several movers, contact your local branch of the Federal Highway Administration's Office of Motor Carriers or your state public utilities commission, transportation department, or consumer affairs office. Ask if they have received any complaints and confirm that the companies are licensed movers.

- Then it's time to get back on the phone and set up appointments for movers to come to your home and give you an estimate.

Getting an Estimate

Get estimates from at least three moving companies. Allow two hours for each appointment. They will want to look through every room in the house.

Before the moving company representatives arrive, make a list of what services you want them to provide (see Moving Services Checklist on page 4). When you talk with each mover, ask for an estimate based on the same services. This way you get an accurate comparison. Have them itemize the individual charges (i.e., for packing, car transport, stairs), so you can evaluate the mover's prices on each item. You may choose one mover for its overall service record, while hiring a specialist to move your car or custom crate your valuables at a better price.

Answer these questions before you meet with the movers:

◎ What are you taking and what are you leaving behind? List major appliances and large furniture that you plan to move. Will you need appliance servicing? Or will you disconnect and prepare these for the move yourself? Will any of the furniture need to be dismantled?

◎ Do you want the mover to do your packing? Unpacking? Part of it? Do you need to buy any packing supplies, such as boxes and wrapping paper?

◎ Do you want custom crating for fragile or valuable objects, such as paintings, antiques, or chandeliers?

◎ Are you moving a piano, big-screen television, pool table?

◎ Do you want them to move your car or boat? Will you need your car transported with the rest of your possessions or can you wait a couple of weeks for it to arrive on a car carrier?

◎   Will you need storage-in-transit for some or all of your goods? Will you be moving to a temporary residence until a new home is ready and need to be moved again then?

◎   Will the mover encounter any special challenges at the new house? Is the street especially narrow or lacking adequate parking? Is there a long walkway to the house, stairs, a tight corner, an elevator?

◎   What are your scheduling limitations?

◎   What kind of liability protection do you want?

Binding vs. Nonbinding Estimates

There are two main types of estimates: binding and nonbinding. It's to your advantage to get a binding estimate. This is the option most people today choose. Here is how both types work:

◎   With a binding estimate, the mover agrees, in writing, to move you for a fixed price. That price is based on its estimate of the weight of your goods, as well as the distance involved, and any additional charges. No matter what your load actually weighs on the day of the move, you will pay this amount. (Unless, of course, you add or delete items being moved or make another change in service.) Binding estimates are typically good for sixty days.

A mover may be reluctant to give you a binding estimate if you are unsure about significant details of the move that would affect price.

◎   A nonbinding estimate does not bind the mover to the estimate. The price tag of the move will be determined by the actual weight of the goods and the distance covered. Your goods are weighed after they are put in the truck, so you don't find out the cost until the move is under way. When the shipment arrives, you are required to pay the amount of the original estimate, plus up to 10 percent more if the cost exceeds the estimate. You have at least thirty days to pay the balance.

If you do end up getting a nonbinding estimate, make sure the mover puts it in writing. The estimate should clearly describe the contents of the shipment and the services to be provided.

◎ One variation of a nonbinding estimate is a "not to exceed" price. You will be charged for the actual weight of your goods and the distance covered, but only up to the "not to exceed" price. This establishes a ceiling for the charge.

Negotiations

When talking with the moving company representatives, set out all the terms you want met in the move.

◎ Find out what kind of schedule they can offer for packing, loading, and delivery.

◎ Ask if movers can cover carpets, banisters, and traffic areas with protective material on the day of the move to prevent damage.

◎ Inquire about the types of liability coverage available. Make sure they clearly understand everything you want moved.

◎ Tell the representatives that you are getting several estimates and are comparing prices. Ask them for a discount on services.

◎   Each representative will then prepare an estimate for you. Special services, such as packing and unpacking, appliance servicing, and the shipment of an automobile, should be included in the estimate.

If you get a lower bid from one company, call your first-choice company and see if they will match or better the other bid.

Choosing a Mover

In selecting a mover, your decision should be based not just on price, but on the company's reputation, performance record, and service offerings.

◎   The company should be operating with a business permit and be adequately insured.

◎   Your local Better Business Bureau may be helpful in weeding out bad apples.

◎   If your state has licensing requirements, contact your state public utilities commission to make sure the company is licensed and has not been the subject of complaints.

◎   If you're moving out of the state, find out if the company is federally licensed by contacting your local branch of the Federal Highway Administration's Office of Motor Carriers.

◎   If you are planning to use a national van line, keep in mind that each of its agents, or local offices, operates independently. When choosing your moving company, look not only at the reputation of the parent company, but at the reputation of the local agent. Performance records can vary.

◎   Pay attention to the way the company has treated you

so far. Have representatives answered all of your questions willingly and in a straightforward manner? Have they behaved professionally and treated you with courtesy?

◎   Confirm that they belong to an arbitration plan. This federal requirement is designed to protect you in the event of a dispute over damages.

Once you make your choice, keep in close contact with the company to confirm dates and service. Let them know that you expect the best treatment. Don't hesitate to complain to your company moving representative if you are not getting it.

Order for Service

◎   The order for service is the document authorizing the van line to perform moving services. Movers are required to prepare an order for service on every shipment for an individual and you are entitled to a copy. It should specify the estimated price and the spread of days on which the moving van will pick up and deliver your goods. It will also list other details of your move: addresses, phone numbers, special services, liability coverage selected, and the method of payment.

Changes or Cancellation

◎   If you add items or request services not included in the estimate, the carrier will provide a change order for services. Confirm that the mover has figured the new price using the agreed-upon discounts. Make sure the form is filled out before you sign it and keep a copy for your records.

◎   An order for service is not a contract. You can cancel
or postpone service at any point if your plans change. As
a courtesy, call to notify the company as soon as you
can.

Scheduling

◎   Typically, interstate movers agree to pick up and
deliver your goods within a "spread" of anywhere
from two to four days on both ends. This could mean
they agree to arrive at your old home on a Friday or
Saturday and deliver your belongings on the following
Wednesday, Thursday, Friday, or Saturday. Be sure
to get the dates in writing on your order for service.

◎   Deliveries are handled this way because van drivers
usually combine several shipments on the same trip,
which may impact their delivery schedule. You can pay
an extra fee to request specific pickup or delivery dates,
make space reservations, or be the only shipment on the
truck.

◎   Moving companies must pick up and deliver your
goods on the days specified, unless circumstances that
are out of their control arise to prevent this. They
should notify you as soon as possible of any delays.

◎   Many of the large moving companies will give consumers cash reimbursements if there is a delay. These
are known as delay claims or inconvenience claims and
they range from $100 to $125 a day. As with a binding
estimate, you must specifically request this option; in
many cases there is no additional charge. You may also
be eligible for further damages.

Protection for Your Goods

When the mover representative is in your home to prepare the estimate, this is also the time to discuss liability coverage. This is temporary protection for your goods, which may not be covered by your homeowner's insurance policy while they are in transit.

Interstate movers are liable for any loss or damage to your property, but there are different levels of liability. Make sure you understand the protection provided by the policy you choose. There are three basic types:

- ◎ Replacement value protection coverage, or R.V.P., offers the most protection. Unless your goods are covered under a separate insurance policy *(confirm this with your agent; don't assume)*, you may want to consider this plan.

    R.V.P. offers full replacement value for your possessions. Should you experience the loss of or damage to any of your possessions, the company will repair or replace the item or pay you cash for it, based on what it would cost to buy it today.

    The cost and protection level of the coverage is determined by the value you declare for your shipment. You can get full coverage with no deductible or you can reduce the cost of the insurance by opting for a deductible, typically $250 or $500.

- ◎ Declared value protection coverage (D.V.P.), also referred to as actual cash value coverage, is the middle level of protection. Unless you specify another type of coverage, your goods are automatically covered under this plan by law. The mover may also automatically charge you a set fee ($7.00 at this writing) per $1,000 of coverage. This plan is less than ideal for most people, because it reimburses you for the item at its depreciated or actual market value rate. This is usually much less than it would cost you to replace the item.

If you opt for this coverage (if only through default), the mover is required to assume liability for the entire shipment at a depreciated amount equal to $1.25 per pound times the weight of your shipment. If your shipment weighs 4,000 pounds, for example, the mover will be liable to you for loss or damage up to $5,000. This would be the ceiling whether your claim was for one item or the entire shipment.

You can buy additional protection from the mover under this plan by declaring a specific dollar value for your shipment, as long as it exceeds the $1.25 per pound figure. You may, for example, declare that your 4,000-pound shipment is worth $10,000.

◎ Basic liability protection or "released value" coverage insures your belongings at the rate of $.60 per pound per item, regardless of their actual value. That means a claim for a lost or damaged television set weighing 10 pounds would be settled for $6.00. This protection is included in the mover's fee. You must specify that you want this level of insurance by writing it into the bill of lading, otherwise you will be charged for declared value protection, explained above.

People sometimes take the basic liability protection when they are purchasing a separate insurance rider for their goods so they will not be charged twice.

One more point: Always itemize objects whose value exceeds $100 per pound on your inventory sheet, and declare their value. Otherwise the mover is allowed by law to limit its liability for loss or damage to these items. It is not a good idea to include jewelry and important documents in your shipment.

Packing

- Find out how many packers will be assisting you. They often work in pairs, but a larger house might justify more helpers.

- Ask your moving company how it handles items such as antiques and crystal to determine if you might prefer to move valuables yourself or ship them by another method.

- You may wish to save money by packing your own household goods. Be aware that if you file a claim for breakage, you will have to show the damage occurred because of the mover's negligent handling and not your packing. The company may not insure or take responsibility for items they did not pack. Confirm the company's policy beforehand. If there is damage, always save the box, the contents, and the packing materials to support your claim.

- Professional packers are famous for packing everything, including unwashed breakfast dishes and trash cans filled with garbage. Have your house in order and ready to pack before they arrive.

- Clearly label boxes with the room where they should be taken when unloaded.

- Prominently label DO NOT PACK or set aside in a safe place items that should not be packed. When you're walking through the house with packers, point these out. Also note the items that you want in boxes labeled LOAD LAST, UNLOAD FIRST or DO NOT UNPACK.

◎ It is your responsibility to disconnect major appliances and secure them for the move, and remove items
such as draperies and carpets that are attached to walls
or floors. Some moving companies provide these services for a fee or can recommend other firms.

Moving Day

On the days of the move and delivery, the person
often in charge is the driver, also known as the van foreman. The driver is responsible for loading your belongings,
driving them to your new home in the van, and delivering
them intact. Establish a good rapport with this important
person!

Inventory Report

The driver will prepare an inventory of your possessions before loading anything onto the truck. In addition
to tagging every individual carton or piece of furniture
with numbered and color-coded labels, the driver records
each item on the inventory form, with a description of any
existing damage.

◎ Go over the driver's inventory list to make sure everything is on the list and that you are in agreement about
the condition of your belongings. If you disagree, make
your own notation on the inventory list. Otherwise you
may have difficulty securing compensation should damage occur.
◎ When you sign the inventory, you are indicating that
the pieces were loaded and that you agree with the
driver's description of their condition before the move.

The driver will sign the form as well and present you with a copy. Keep this inventory with you for use on delivery day.

Bill of Lading

The driver will ask you to sign a bill of lading. This is a legal contract authorizing the van line to transport your possessions and saying that you agree to pay for those services. The bill of lading confirms the services the mover will provide, pickup and delivery schedules, and the valuation and protection plan that you've selected. The details on the bill of lading should agree with the details on the order for service and the estimate.

◉ You must sign this document before the movers begin loading. Keep it in a safe place with the rest of your moving documents. You'll need it when your goods are delivered and for any claims you may file against the mover.

  If you cannot be present at the time of loading, you need to arrange for a responsible person to act as your agent in signing both the bill of lading and the inventory sheet.

Loading

◉ Ask that the movers use floor runners to protect carpets and flooring in entryways, hallways, and other high-traffic areas and padding on banisters and doorways to avoid marring walls and woodwork. Furniture

should be wrapped with cloth pads or blankets to protect it.

◎   Treat the movers like professionals. Be on the scene,
but don't follow their every move. If you did your own
packing, the driver or his helper may ask you to open a
carton for inspection before loading it on the truck.

◎   After everything has been loaded in the van, it's a
good idea for you and the van foreman to take one last
walk through your house to make sure nothing has been
overlooked.

Weighing Your Shipment

If your charges are based on the weight of the shipment, as they are in a nonbinding estimate, the mover is
required to weigh the shipment and you are allowed to
observe the weighings. (If you would like to do so, tell
your representative before the move.) Drivers may weigh
goods by one of two methods:

◎   In "origin" weighing, the driver will weigh the truck
before coming to your residence and then again after
loading. The difference between the two weights is the
weight of your shipment.

◎   "Destination" weighing works in reverse order as origin weighing. The mover weighs the load immediately
before and after unloading your goods. Again, the difference in these two weights is the amount for which
you will be charged.

◎   The driver must attach a copy of the weight ticket
when presenting your freight bill to you upon delivery.
This ticket must show the date and place of weighing
and the weight obtained, as well as your name and ship-

ment number and the I.D. number of the truck. If you doubt the accuracy of the weight, you may ask to have the shipment reweighed before unloading, at no extra charge to you.

Payment

Contact your destination agent as soon as you arrive in your new town so that final delivery arrangements can be made. If you do not show up on the agreed-upon delivery day, the mover may put your things in storage and charge you for it.

◎ When the moving van arrives at your new home, be ready to pay the moving charges with cash, money order, traveler's check, or cashier's check. Personal checks are usually not accepted. Unless approved billing or credit arrangements have been made in advance, the driver is required to collect the payment for your move before your shipment can be unloaded. If your shipment is placed in storage, charges up to that point are due. The bill of lading is your receipt for payment.

◎ You are required on the day of the delivery to pay the amount of the original estimate, plus up to 10 percent more if the nonbinding estimate was low. One way to handle this is to get a cashier's check or money order for the amount of the estimate. Then have on hand enough traveler's checks in a variety of denominations to cover the extra 10 percent. Or you can arrange in advance to have the driver notify you of the charges before delivery.

◎ You have at least thirty days to pay the balance of the amount over the estimate.

Delivery

◉ Unloading will go faster if you have a furniture floor plan in mind. Draw up floor plans for each room and post them for everyone to see. Or tell the driver where you want things placed as they are unloaded and brought into your home.

◉ The driver and crew should reassemble any items, such as beds, that they took apart at your old home.

◉ As the driver unloads boxes and furniture, take note of their condition. If anything is missing or damaged, mark this on both the driver's and your copy of the inventory list. Inspect cartons carrying china, glassware, and other fragile items for damage before the carrier leaves. You need not unpack every box, but you should note if a box seems damaged. Also write down any items that are unaccounted for. The claims process is easier when you do this. Whether you do or don't, however, you will still be eligible to have a claim considered.

◉ If you discover broken items after the movers have left, keep them in the original box. Contact your moving agent as soon as possible.

◉ If you want movers to unpack your boxes and take away the empties, be sure to request this service before the move. Your moving counselor will add the extra fee onto your estimate. Should you do the unpacking yourself, you will be responsible for getting rid of the empty cartons and used materials.

Legal Protections

Everyone has heard the horror stories of rude and irresponsible workers, companies that delivered later than promised, and belongings that were damaged or destroyed.

You can avoid these problems by knowing the regulations that are in place to protect you and making sure your company abides by them. FHWA requires that movers:

◉   give you an order for service. It must have on it the estimated price of the move and the dates the moving van will pick up and deliver (it can specify a span of days).

◉   send the moving van on the day or span of days promised unless circumstances out of their control prevent it. They must notify you of any delays and tell you at that time when your shipment will be delivered.

◉   deliver your goods and do anything else requested, such as putting the furniture where you want it, putting things back together, and unpacking, if you pay the required amount.

◉   itemize the cost of packing and unpacking separately on the bill. You need not pay for unpacking unless you have ordered it. If you have ordered it and the mover refuses to do it, you are entitled to a refund.

◉   give you the company's performance record for the previous year when the representative comes to your house to do an estimate. When you talk with more than one company, you can compare performance records. Keep in mind that the company works through an independent local agent, which may have its own record.

Filing a Claim

If you find anything that has been lost or damaged, you have up to nine months to file a claim. However, the sooner you file it the better. If you do not file your claim within 120 days following a delivery and later bring a legal action against the mover to recover damages, you may not be able to recover your attorney fees even though you win the court action.

- ◉ All claims must be in writing. Obtain a claim form from the carrier's nearest agent. Include your order-for-service number on any paperwork regarding your claim. The carrier must acknowledge your claim within 30 days and respond within 120 days either by paying or denying the claim or proposing a compromise settlement.
- ◉ If you and the carrier cannot reach agreement, you may be eligible for arbitration administered by the American Arbitration Association. More information on this program is available from the American Movers Conference, 1611 Duke Street, Alexandria, Virginia 22314; (703) 683-7410 (phone), or (703) 683-7527 (fax).

Take these precautions to better your chances of recovering damages:

- ◉ Be sure any losses or damages you find are clearly noted on the van foreman's inventory sheet before you sign it. It's not necessary to unpack every box immediately, but do look for obvious damage to cartons.
- ◉ Maintain damaged items in their shipping boxes and do not dispose of any broken or chipped pieces until after your claim has been settled.
- ◉ Safeguard your copy of all paperwork for future reference.
- ◉ If you have items that are unusual in nature or value, have them appraised before your move.

Common Moving Terms

To negotiate properly with your mover, it helps to be speaking the same language. Here are some terms your mover may use:

- **Accessorial services:** Services besides transportation that you get from your mover for an additional charge, such as packing and unpacking, storage-in-transit.
- **Agent:** Local moving company representing a national van line. Could be the booking, origin, destination, or hauling agent.
- **Appliance servicing:** Services to prepare major appliances for the move, performed at an extra charge.
- **Bill of lading:** Important receipt the driver gives you in exchange for your belongings on the day of the move. It serves as a contract for the move.
- **Booking agent:** Agent or person who sells you the move and registers it with the van line.
- **Change order:** Form used to make a change to the amount on the original estimate when you add or delete items or request changes in service.
- **Destination agent:** Local agent who provides services and information at the end of your move.
- **Estimate:** Price the company estimates it would charge for preparing and moving your belongings. The mover bases this on the estimated weight of the goods and distance of the move.
- **Hauling agent:** Agent or driver who owns the van assigned by the van line to move your possessions.
- **Inventory:** Form on which the van driver lists each item in your shipment and describes its pre-move condition.
- **Moving counselor:** Agent's sales representative who

provides the estimate and oversees the move on the starting end.

◎ **Order for service:** Once you have agreed to work with a company, this document authorizes the van line to perform moving services. It is not a contract for services; you can cancel at any time.

◎ **Origin agent:** Agent who is responsible for performing, packing, and preparing necessary documentation.

◎ **Registration number:** Number assigned by the van line to identify your shipment. It is printed in the upper-right-hand corner of the order for service and the bill of lading.

◎ **Storage-in-transit:** Temporary storage of not more than ninety days for your household goods.

◎ **Van line:** National moving company through which affiliated agents are granted the authority to transport interstate shipments. The van line handles dispatching, shipment routing and monitoring, paperwork processing, and claims settlement for all interstate shipments handled by its agents.

◎ **Van foreman:** Van driver responsible for loading, transporting, and unloading your belongings.

Local Moves

For local moves, some people prefer to use a national mover with a recognized name and reputation, rather than a smaller company they've heard nothing about. However, the service you get from an independent mover can be just as good or even better than that of a big-name mover. The key is to ask the right questions when you are making your selection, so you know what you're getting.

Much of the same advice given in the previous section on using interstate movers applies to using local movers. But because there is less danger in transporting goods three miles than there is in moving them thirty thousand miles, you may find a much more casual approach among local companies than among interstate movers. Here are some areas where local service differs.

How They Charge

◎ For local moves, moving companies will charge you by the hour and by distance. The hourly rate varies according to the number of workers they send. For example, if one worker is enough to handle your move, the hourly rate might be $50 an hour. If two workers come to your house—which is more standard—the rate might go up to $70 or $75 an hour, and so on.

◎ In addition, time spent on the road, transporting your goods from your old to your new home, is typically charged at double the hourly rate. A one-hour drive, for example, would be billed at two hours. This is to compensate the movers for the time it takes them to get back to the starting point of the move.

◎ Be sure to ask when the mover starts the time clock. If it's from the time the van leaves the company warehouse, rather than when the movers arrive at your home, you'll want to choose a mover located near your home.

◎ If you have only a few things to move, be aware that some carriers may have minimum charges. That means that the carrier may charge you its four-hour minimum, even if your move only takes three.

◎ When you move within the state, but out of the local area, it is considered a long-distance move. As with an interstate move, you will be charged according to the weight of the shipment and distance.

Getting an Estimate

Always get several estimates. While some local movers will come to your home to give you a written estimate, others may want to give you a ballpark figure or quote you an hourly rate over the phone. Remember that you always have more protection with a written estimate. Get as much in writing as you can—the date and time of the move, the hourly rate, the "not to exceed" fee, the size of the truck, and the number of workers. The fewer surprises the better.

Liability Protection

Although there is less risk to your goods than on a long-distance move because you are always nearby, be sure to ask about liability protection. Are they self-insured or covered by a major carrier? Do they offer replacement value protection? Ask your insurance agent about protection against loss while your belongings are in transit; you may be able to get a rider on your homeowner's policy to cover losses.

Choosing a Mover

Local or "intrastate" movers are not regulated nationally, so it falls to individual states to monitor their work. Some states do not have any consumer protections regarding moving; others place strict regulations on movers.

- Contact your state consumer affairs office or public utilities commission to find out what kinds of regulations apply to movers in your state. Ask if there is a licensing requirement for movers in your state. (Typically, this means they must pass a test, show proof of insurance, and meet certain regulations.) Have them send you their guidelines for selecting and working with a mover in your state.

- When you have narrowed the field to a couple of movers, check with the state agency to be sure the companies are licensed and that there have been no complaints filed against them.

- Check with your local Better Business Bureau office or consumer group to get any additional information.

- Visit the mover's place of business. What is the condition of the facility and of its trucks? Are they rundown?

Clean and well-maintained? This may reflect on how they will treat you and your belongings.

Moving Day

◎ On the day of the move, make sure you get a written contract—and read it carefully before signing it. It should spell out all of the terms of the move, including your name, new address and telephone number, and the agreed-upon price. Be sure you have a phone number for the mover and the I.D. number of the truck.

◎ Many local companies do not provide a written inventory of your goods unless you ask for it. Some may want to charge you for the time it takes to prepare it. This may be worth the small price you pay.

Do-It-Yourself Moves

W hen most people choose to move their own belongings, it's because they're on a budget and have more time than money to spare.

A do-it-yourself move can cost virtually nothing. It can be as basic as packing the contents of your dorm room into your car and taking off. Or borrowing a friend's truck and moving everything in your house over a weekend. It can also be a bigger production: renting a large moving van and accessories from a truck rental company and recruiting friends or paying assistants to help with the work.

Some people go with a DIY (do-it-yourself) move because they want to be able to move at their own convenience, rather than having to work around a mover's schedule. Others like the control of knowing exactly how their belongings will be handled.

A DIY move is a good choice if you're moving a relatively small amount of goods a short distance. Think twice, though, if yours is a large household. Moving a large household can be an exhausting task best left to the pros. And for long-distance moves, vehicle rental charges combined with the cost of gasoline (trucks get just five to eight

miles per gallon) and the stress of driving may tip the
balance toward hiring a professional.

Do consider a DIY move if you:

◎ are moving locally;
◎ know people willing to help you or people you can
   hire;
◎ are in good physical condition;
◎ have access to and are comfortable driving a large
   truck.

DIY may not be for you if you:

◎ are without adequate help;
◎ own heavy furniture, valuable antiques, or large appliances;
◎ are prone to back trouble;
◎ are moving a long distance.

Renting a Truck

Unless you own very few possessions, have a good
friend with a big truck, or possess the patience for making
numerous trips in the car, you will need to rent a truck or
van to move your belongings.

Make your reservations early, a full month in advance
of your move if possible. This is especially true in the peak
months of May through October, on weekends, and at the
beginning or end of the month when many people move.
You may be able to get a truck or trailer with two weeks or
less notice, but why take a chance with availability?

What They Charge

Rental rates vary, so shop around for the best prices. Companies will charge you in one of two ways.

◉   There are local or round-trip moves, where you return the truck to the same location. Charges are based on a standard day rate and the mileage you incur.

◉   In long-distance or one-way moves, companies typically charge a flat rate, based on the size of the vehicle and your destination.

Either way, you will be required to pay a sizable deposit in cash or with a credit card. This will be refunded when you return the truck, minus whatever charges you have incurred.

Quotes do not include extras such as dollies, furniture pads, boxes, packing materials, and comprehensive insurance.

When figuring the price, remember to factor in the cost of gasoline, which can be high because of the low mileage. You can estimate the fuel charge by dividing the number of miles you are traveling by the miles per gallon you get in the truck. Then multiply the number of gallons by the price per gallon of gas.

Making Your Selection

Choose a company based on several criteria: cost, condition of vehicles, availability, liability coverage, and the company's repair policy in case of breakdown. Will the company send someone out to repair or replace the truck? Ask whether its vehicles have standard or automatic transmission, so you won't be surprised on the day of the move.

How Much Truck Do You Need?

Use the Inventory Checklist on page 71 to figure out the total cubic footage of your goods. Compare that figure to the list of truck sizes below to determine exactly what size truck you will need.

◎ For more general estimates, you can figure the truck size by considering the number of rooms in the house. Professionals estimate that you need 150 cubic feet of cargo space for the average room in your house. If you are debating one size truck over another, it's better to err on the side of having more room than you need rather than cutting it too close to save a few dollars.

◎ On moving day, if you find that you've underestimated your space needs, all is not lost. You can always rent a trailer and attach it to the back of the truck to carry the items that didn't fit.

Truck rental companies offer a variety of van sizes. Here are some typical sizes and the amount of cargo they hold:

◎ Trailers attach to the back of your vehicle with a tow bar provided by the rental company. These come in different sizes. Use a trailer to move the contents of two rooms, a studio apartment, a dorm room, or just a few items. They hold from about 80 to 470 cubic feet of cargo.

◎ A ten-foot cargo van is not much bigger than a large trailer. Use it for a studio apartment or two rooms. It holds 400 cubic feet of cargo, or 3,000 pounds.

◎ Use a fifteen-foot midsize truck to move the contents

of a one- to two-bedroom house with two to four rooms. It will hold 750 cubic feet, or 2,600 pounds.

◎ A twenty-foot truck will hold the contents of a three-bedroom house with five to six total rooms. That's 1,250 cubic feet, or 7,000 pounds.

◎ Rent a twenty-four-foot truck for a four-bedroom house with seven to eight rooms. It holds 1,550 cubic feet, or 10,700 pounds.

Inventory Checklist

When you're moving yourself, you need to know the total cubic feet of your belongings to help you decide how large a truck you need. Here is a guide to figuring out how big your shipment will be.

◎ First jot down how many of each type of item you are moving. Then multiply that by the cubic footage of each one. For example, let's say you have four dining room chairs that are each 4 cubic feet. That gives you a total of 16 cubic feet for the dining room chairs.

◎ Next add up the cubic footage of the contents of each room. Finally add the cubic footage of all of the rooms together. This gives you an approximate cubic footage for all of your possessions.

◎ To find the cubic footage of an item not listed in the chart, multiply its length times its width times its depth. The figure you arrive at is its cubic footage.

◎ If you haven't yet packed up your books, dishes, clothes, etc., in boxes, you will have to estimate the amount of space these will take. Always figure on more space rather than less. Better to have extra room in the truck than to not be able to fit everything in.

Room, Item	Cubic feet	Quantity	Total Cubic Feet
Bedrooms			
Bassinet	4		
Bed, single	30		
Bed, double	45		
Bed, queen	55		
Bed, king	75		
Dresser or chest	20		
Cedar chest	10		
Chair, straight	4		
Clothes hamper	3		
Crib	8		
Dresser bench	4		
Night table	4		
Playpen	6		
Rug with pad	8		
Television, portable	8		
Toy chest	4		
Wardrobe or armoire	36		
Boxes			
Other			
Total			
Kitchen/Laundry			
Breakfast table	10		
Chair, straight	4		
Clothes dryer	20		
Dishwasher	15		
High chair	3		
Ironing board	2		
Range	25		
Refrigerator	40		

Room, Item	Cubic feet	Quantity	Total Cubic Feet
Sewing machine (portable)	3		
Sewing machine (upright)	8		
Utility cart	3		
Vacuum cleaner	3		
Washing machine	20		
Boxes			
Other			
Total			
Living Room, Family Room, Den			
Bookcase	12		
Chair, arm	10		
Chair, occasional	14		
Chair, overstuffed recliner	20		
Chair, rocker	12		
Couch, sofa	30		
Desk	20		
Drapes	3		
Floor lamp	3		
Hide-a-bed	35		
Mirror	3		
Rug with pad	80		
Tables, coffee or end	4		
Table lamp	2		
Stereo	2–4		
Television, portable	8		
Television, console	12		

Room, Item	Cubic feet	Quantity	Total Cubic Feet
Boxes			
Other			
Total			
Dining Room			
Buffet	25		
Buffet with hutch top	30		
China cabinet	20		
Corner cupboard	14		
Chair, dining	4		
Table, drop-leaf	14		
Boxes			
Other			
Total			
Garage, Patio, Yard			
Barbecue	5		
Bicycle	6		
Clothes basket	3		
Cot, folding	3		
Fan	1		
Filing cabinet	8		
Garden cart	3		
Garden hose and tools	8		
Golf bag and clubs	2		
Heater	3		
Lawn chair	3		
Lawn mower	5		
Lawn swing	20		
Picnic bench	20		

Room, Item	Cubic feet	Quantity	Total Cubic Feet
Stepladder	5		
Swing set	20		
Tool chest	30		
Tricycle	4		
Wagon	5		
Wheelbarrow	6		
Boxes			
Other			
Total			
Boxes			
Small box	1.5		
Medium box	3		
Large box	4.5		
Dish-pack box	6		
Wardrobe box	13		
Total			
GRAND TOTAL			

Accessories

In addition to the moving van, you'll need other equipment and supplies to transport your belongings.

◎ **Hand truck:** Use this two-wheeled vertical cart for moving heavy appliances or a stack of cartons. Use straps to secure the load.

◎ **Dolly:** You can rent this low platform with wheels to move large and heavy objects.

- **Furniture pads and straps:** Quilted blankets wrap around furniture for protection. You secure them with straps.
- **Tow bar, auto carrier:** Rent one of these devices to tow your car behind the truck. Tow bars or dollies leave wheels on the road; with an auto carrier, the car rides off the ground.
- **Moving ramp:** This attaches to the back of the truck and can be pulled down to make loading easier. It is typically included at no charge.
- **Boxes and materials:** Boxes are available in a wide variety of sizes and for specific purposes, from cushioning mirrors to protecting dishes. You'll also need plastic tape, wrapping paper, and other packing materials. Avoid using printed newspaper to wrap items as it stains.
- **Padlock:** You'll need to bring your own lock to secure the back of the truck.

Calculating Costs

You can estimate the cost of your DIY move by totaling up these items.

ITEM	COST
Truck	_____
Hand trucks	_____
Dollies	_____
Insurance coverage	_____
Furniture pads, straps	_____
Tow bar or auto carrier	_____

Boxes, packing materials	_____
Tax	_____
Gas	_____
Tolls	_____
Lodging	_____
Meals	_____
Other	_____
TOTAL	_____

Protection

Ask rental companies to explain their coverage policies to you when you're making your reservations. Consider getting maximum coverage. The cost is minimal compared to the peace of mind it can bring when driving an unfamiliar vehicle loaded with all of your possessions. Here are some questions you should ask:

◎ If they offer cargo protection for your belongings, how much coverage does the policy provide? What type of coverage?
◎ Are your goods covered in the event of loss or theft— and for how much? Is there an add-on "floater" policy for valuables?
◎ Is there medical coverage for you and your helpers?
◎ How about for other people in the event of an accident?

If you are responsible for physical damage to the vehicle, consider getting the physical damage waiver. It may be worth the expense.

Check with your insurance broker to find out what

your current automobile and homeowner's policies cover when you are renting a moving vehicle. Can a rider offering extra protection be added to the policy?

Helpers

You may be able to recruit helpers among your friends and family. Get definite commitments from people and a clear agreement as to what time they will show up, how long they will work, and what kind of help they will provide. (Be honest about the size of the job. If you need them to help move a houseful of heavy oak furniture, tell them!)

In exchange for their help, provide generous quantities of food and drinks for the day. Keep an eye on the beer consumption until the job is finished. By no means let anyone who has been drinking drive. Keep your cool and try to make the day as pleasant as possible for everyone. Remember to say thank you when the day is over.

You can also hire workers to help with the task. Are you acquainted with any energetic college or high school students who might like to make some extra money? Ask people you know for recommendations or check local newspaper classified ads and bulletin boards.

Loading the Truck

◉   Park the truck with the loading door facing as close as possible to your home. Pull out the loading ramp and place it on the highest step to your home that it can reach.

◉   Load the truck one quarter at a time, packing it solidly from floor to ceiling. Fill open spaces with small boxes. Secure each quarter of the load with rope or straps that attach to the side of the truck.

◎ Load the largest and heaviest items, such as appliances, first. Large furniture goes in next. Putting the heavy weight up front is essential to keeping the vehicle stable when you're driving.

◎ Long items, including mattresses, box springs, sofas, and tabletops, should be placed on their sides against truck walls and tied down. Mirrors should stand upright. Never lay them flat. To protect them, tie them to truck walls or place them between mattresses and box springs.

◎ Pack heavy boxes on bottom and lighter boxes on top of them. You can stack heavy boxes on top of each other if they're about the same weight.

◎ Put other odd-shaped pieces along the walls or on top of the load. Wrap pads around all delicate items.

◎ Secure and tie down the load and lock the truck.

Lifting

◎ When lifting heavy objects, bend your knees and squat down in front of the box, with your left foot on the side of the box and right foot in front of it. Grab the right bottom corner of the box with your right hand and, diagonal to that, the left side with your left hand. Get up by lifting the weight with your leg muscles, rising with your back straight, holding the weight close to your body.

◎ Do not lift more than you can comfortably handle.

◎ Always pull, rather than push, the hand truck up the ramp.

Driving Tips

Familiarize yourself with the moving van before you get on the road. Look over gauges, switches, and other controls so you know where they are before you start driving. Adjust the seat and mirrors. Check all the seatbelts.

Driving a large truck takes some getting used to. Before you load your belongings, spend some time driving around and getting accustomed to the truck's feel and dimensions. Practice parking, changing lanes, backing up, and merging onto the freeway. If the truck is a standard transmission vehicle, get comfortable shifting gears, especially when driving up hills and in parallel parking situations. Test out the brakes and note how long it takes to stop.

◉   Take everything slowly—starting, driving, and stopping. Don't race down city streets; the impact of an unexpected dip in the road is magnified in a big truck carrying your precious household goods. This is not the time to run yellow lights. Here are a few other things to keep in mind as you drive.

◉   Find out exactly how high the vehicle is and keep clearance levels in mind at all times. Watch out for tunnels, tree branches, street decorations, and gas station overhangs.

◉   A truck accelerates much more slowly than a car. Allow more time to merge with traffic and to pass. Never pass a vehicle doing more than 40 m.p.h. and do not pass on hills or curves.

◉   Do not make abrupt lane changes. Use your turn signals and make sure other drivers see you before you move over.

◎   Slow down into turns and curves. You don't want to send your furniture or goods flying or lose control of the vehicle.

◎   There are different speed limits for trucks than for cars on some roads; pay attention to the signs.

◎   It takes longer to stop a truck, so allow plenty of stopping distance. Never tailgate. Don't overrely on the brakes to slow down. Anticipate stops and slow down by downshifting and braking.

◎   Always park with the engine off, the transmission in "park" or in gear, the parking brake on and the wheels turned toward the curb.

◎   Be aware of other drivers around you and give them the right of way; trucks take up more room in the lane. Use your headlights at dusk to increase visibility.

On the Road

When you're ready to leave on your trip, stow your important papers and valuables in a safe place or lock them away in the back of the truck. Put your travel kit and personal suitcase aside as well. Keep an ice chest filled with food and beverages handy.

Remember that safety is the first and most important rule. Always keep your seatbelt on and instruct everyone else in the truck to do the same. If you need to refer to a map, let someone else do the navigating while you keep your eyes on the road. Never drink and drive. When you find yourself getting tired, pull over at a rest stop and take a break.

If you're driving a long distance, pay attention to gas, oil, and water levels. Also check tire air pressure. Wash the windshield frequently. Check the load from time to time to make sure nothing has shifted.

Road Emergencies

If there is a problem, pull your truck onto the shoulder of the road, as far over as you safely can. Turn on your flashers and pull out the reflectors.

Many companies have a toll-free number you can call in case of breakdown. They may offer to send a mechanic out to fix the problem or bring a replacement truck. When you're shopping around for companies, find out about their policy on breakdowns.

Unloading

◎ When you arrive at your new home, get out and stretch. You've made it!

◎ Park the truck with the loading door facing as close as possible to your new home. Pull out the loading ramp and place it on the house's highest step.

◎ Walk through the house and turn on lights, checking to see what utilities are working.

◎ Unload the truck. As you're unloading, check all items against your inventory list. Carry boxes to the room in which they belong.

◎ When you're finished, check every corner of the truck's cab and cargo space to make sure it's empty. Return it and settle your bill.

Towing Your Car

Towing your car behind the truck will slow you down and decrease mileage. Still, it may be the best or least expensive way to get your car to your new home. Truck rental companies rent out tow bars or tow dollies that attach your car to the back of the truck. Some offer car carriers, trailers attached to the rear of the truck on which your car rides.

Shipping Services

❂ ❂ ❂ ❂

Instead of using a mover, you may be able to save money and time by shipping some or all of your belongings by mail, packaging or express service, air, train, or bus. This is especially true if you have a small load that doesn't meet the mover's minimum weight. These methods work best for boxes rather than furniture. In all cases, insurance coverage is available at a price. Be sure to get details on the type of coverage and the procedure for recovering losses.

Shipping by Mail

⦿ You can mail books, records, videotapes, and cassettes by the special fourth-class book rate for much less than it costs to have them moved. Boxes must be no larger than 108 inches total in the length and width, and weigh no more than 70 pounds.

⦿ Mailing by regular fourth class, or parcel post, is a good way to transport bulky or light items. Packages will take up to two weeks to get to the destination and the price is the same no matter where they're going.

◎   Registered mail can be used to ship valuables that you don't want to take with you on the trip. Delivery takes up to three days. You can mail the package to your new home if you will be there to sign for it. Or you can mail it to yourself care of general delivery at the post office nearest your new home. While packages mailed this way are not inexpensive, the advantage is that you can insure them for large amounts.

Packing and Shipping Services

You can also transport your goods through a packaging or express delivery, or a parcel shipping company. Many have local franchises in neighborhood mail centers. For a small fee, they pick up your goods, package and crate them at their warehouse, and then ship them to your destination.

You may see some savings over moving company prices by using a shipper, particularly if you are moving heavy items, such as books or tools. But convenience is the big factor. Instead of a lengthy pickup and delivery spread, many services will make an appointment for a specific pickup time, ship your goods cross-country to your home within a few days, and set up an appointment for delivery, too.

Shipping by Air

If you're planning to fly to your destination, take advantage of the baggage allowance to transport some of your goods. Typically each person can carry one or two bags onto the plane and check two to three additional pieces of luggage weighing under 70 pounds each; you can pay a small fee to add another heavy bag. Multiply this per-person allowance by the number of people traveling in your group. If you're a family of four, that's nearly 600 pounds of luggage you didn't have to pay a mover to transport.

◉ If you want to transport large shipments, send your goods separately, or to move things overseas, contact the airline cargo division. Airlines will accept everything from individual boxes to entire pallets of goods as air freight. The price decreases with the size of the load. You drop it off and pick it up again at the airline cargo area.

Shipping by Bus

Buses are useful for transporting large boxes. Pricing is by weight and distance. The box must fit under the bus and weigh 100 pounds or less. Bus companies do not accept fragile items, such as dishes or electronics. Shipping across the country takes less than four days. You drop off and pick up your goods at the bus line's package terminal.

Shipping by Rail

Railroads also charge by weight and distance and the price goes down with larger shipments. The cost can be very reasonable. You drop everything off at one terminal and pick it up at the other. Rail lines accept nothing perishable or breakable, no furniture or appliances; call to get the complete list of what can be shipped. The maximum package is four cubic feet and no more than 100 pounds.

Shipping by Boat

If you're moving overseas, this is the most cost-efficient way to get your goods there. However, your household goods will be in transit from four to eight weeks.

◉ International moving companies can handle all the travel arrangements for you, including paperwork, packing, shipping, and door-to-door delivery. A company representative will come to your home and calculate charges based on estimated weight, size, and density of your goods.

◉ Or you can use a freight forwarder, who will pick up your goods, crate them, and transport them overseas. (Most hire subcontractors to do some of the work.) You are responsible for doing your own paperwork, getting everything through customs, and hiring a mover on the other end to pick up the goods at the dock. Packing is not included unless otherwise requested.

Moving Your Car

◉ ◉ ◉ ◉

When it comes to moving your car or another vehicle, you have several choices. If you are using an interstate mover, you can have the car loaded in the van behind your goods. This is the fastest and most convenient, but also the most expensive route to take.

◉ Your mover can arrange to have your car transported on a car carrier, one of those long ramplike trucks that also carry new cars. This takes more time, but costs less.

◉ You may want to call around on your own and look into independent auto transport companies; there are many from which to choose. Moving a car is a big expense, so it's worth it to do your homework and check around.

◉ If you are driving a rental truck, you can attach the car to the truck and tow it behind you.

◉ You can register the car with an auto drive-away agency and let someone else drive it for you. However there's a risk involved because you don't have any control over who will be driving your car.

Storage

H ave to be out of your old house, but still looking for a new one? You will most likely have to put your belongings into temporary storage and move them again when your new house is ready. Most large moving companies have their own warehouse facilities and can hold your shipment for ninety days or less for a fee. They call this storage-in-transit. When you're ready to make the final leg of the journey, the movers load the whole cargo back on a van and deliver it to your new house.

Or perhaps you're looking for an independent storage facility where you can leave some of your goods for a longer period of time.

- Shop around and compare rates.
- Ask about their record of theft and damage.
- If at all possible, visit the facility to see that it is clean, well-maintained, and secure.
- How accessible would your storage space be—can you drive up to the stall or is it located on a top floor in a warehouse? Inquire about insurance coverage.

Moving Consultants

W hen you don't have the time or energy to oversee the move yourself, but you do have the cash, consider hiring a moving consultant. These super-organizers can handle the moving process from start to finish. Their services include everything from sorting through your possessions and discarding unneeded items to sending address change cards, interviewing movers and getting estimates, handling the utilities, overseeing the packing (while you're on vacation or at work), loading, unpacking and organizing your new home. Charges are calculated by the hour or as a flat fee. Look for moving specialists in the Yellow Pages under "Moving Services" or in newspaper classified ads.

Garage Sales

Having a garage sale prior to your move makes good financial sense. You'll make money on the sale—and save money by moving fewer items.

Timing

Have your sale on a weekend when the weather is mild. Hold a two-day sale if you have enough merchandise. Be sure to have extra help on both days to provide relief when you need to take a break.

What to Sell

Toss out garbage and broken items. Other than that, anything goes. Your junk may be someone else's treasure. Think about what items might be unnecessary in your new home. A power lawn mower will go unused if you're moving to a Manhattan town house. Some items cost more to move than to replace. Firewood is too heavy to move. Sell houseplants if you are moving a long distance.

Pricing

A garage sale is not the way to get full value for a valuable bedroom set or antique necklace. Even if an item cost $50 new and you bought it just last year, you will probably get less than $10 for it. You're not going to make a lot of money on any one item, but the accumulation of fifty-cent items will net you a nice sum for the day.

The price you'll be able to get depends on its condition, current popularity, and age. Look at what's in vogue at the time—a certain period style, type of jewelry, or collectible—and price accordingly. Most items will only fetch a few dollars, some only a quarter or dime.

Put prices on all items, but be willing to negotiate—people expect it.

One easy way to price items is to tag them with color-coded adhesive dots. One color represents fifty cents, another a dollar, and so on. Mark a sheet with the color dots and their price values and post it where it can be easily seen.

At the end of the day, price items to sell. Better to get a dollar for something than to have to pack it up again or throw it away.

Advertising

Place a classified ad in local papers, featuring your best and most unusual items. Take advantage of any free advertising in your community—bulletin boards in your supermarket, church, school, or club. Put up signs at nearby street corners a day or two before your sale. Tell all of your friends and neighbors.

Day of the Sale

Keep the setup simple and organized. Arrange tables for your goods so browsers have room to walk. If possible, make an electrical outlet available to test appliances. Hang clothes on portable ironing or display racks or fold them neatly on a table or blanket. Place books in neat rows in shelves or on a table. Shoes and earrings should be in pairs and dishes and glass should be clean.

Set everything up before your advertised opening. Bargain hounds will be there early.

Stock up on change. Secure all cash in a safe place and keep an eye on it at all times. Keep out only enough money to make change and put the rest in the house. Don't accept checks unless you're well-acquainted with the buyer. This is a good time to get rid of your stash of plastic grocery bags; use them to bag goods.

After the sale, pack up whatever hasn't sold and take it to a local charity as a donation. Some charities will send a truck to pick up the goods. Be sure to get a receipt, as your donation may be tax-deductible. If it has no resale value, no one you know wants it, and is inappropriate as a charitable donation, throw it away.

Packing Like a Pro

⊙　　⊙　　⊙　　⊙

Moving can be an expensive proposition. One of the costliest elements is the charge for packing. You can cut your total price tag by up to a third if you do the packing yourself.

One caveat: Check with your moving company or insurance broker to determine their policies on liability when you do the packing. Some will require proof that the box itself was damaged or crushed before they pay a claim.

Consider hiring professionals to pack or custom-crate your fine china, crystal, antiques, and collectibles. Your moving company or a packing and crating company can do the job. Don't forget to have the goods appraised before the move.

A pair of professionals can pack up your house in a day, but it takes longer when you're going through your own belongings. Don't wait until the day before your move. Start with things you don't need, such as the holiday decorations or the camping equipment. Do a little bit at a time, making a final push throughout the last week. This way you won't find yourself frantically throwing pots and pans into boxes at eleven o'clock the night before the move.

Make an Inventory

One way to complete an inventory of everything you own is to do it as you are packing. As you are filling a box, write down each item going into it on your inventory sheet. Assign the box a number and write that down on your inventory sheet, along with the room it goes into. Later you can go through your records and fill in the value of each item and date of purchase. Now label the box with the box number, room, and general contents.

On moving day you can track these boxes as they go on the truck. When your things arrive at your new home, you'll know right away if anything is missing.

Use It or Lose It

One benefit of moving is that it gives you a great excuse to get rid of all the junk you don't need anymore. Is the item worth wrapping, packing, lifting, carrying, transporting, unpacking, washing, and reorganizing? If not, toss it. Every boxful of goods you don't have to move saves you both time and money.

Some people have trouble getting rid of things because they worry they may need or want these things someday. One way to reduce the stress of deciding what you can throw out is to put the items in question into a box and set the box aside. After a week or two, pull the box out and take a fresh look at each item. Did you need or miss it? Will you ever need it? Or is it time to part company?

If you're a "saver" and you haven't pared down in a

while, start this process early. Don't wait until the last couple of weeks before the move when you'll be busy with so many other things you won't be able to spare the time. Sure, a professional organizer would probably be able to whip through your house in a couple of days. But it's different when everything belongs to you. These are more than inanimate objects—they represent memories as well. Give yourself time to sort through them. Invite a friend in to help you if you need an impartial eye.

◎ The kitchen and laundry room are good places to start. Large appliances are typically the most expensive items to move. If any of these appliances is old or not working well either sell it or get rid of it. You can take the money you made from the sale, combine it with the savings from not moving it, and put the total toward a new model.

◎ Do you have any small appliances that seem to do nothing but take up space? Give them to someone who can really use them. What about that overflowing collection of giant souvenir cups, used yogurt containers, and other plastic clutter? Recycle or toss!

◎ If you have a valuable piece of furniture or art that you no longer want, contact an auction house to sell it for you. Or maybe it's appropriate for a resale or pawn shop. If you're hanging on to keepsakes, save only the things that mean the most to you. Don't throw away something that carries a special memory, is valuable, or is a family heirloom, of course. But if you have a cupboard full of chipped thrift store dishes that are of no value to you, get rid of them.

◎ Scan your shelves for those books, CDs, and albums you won't ever look at or listen to again. These are heavy to move! Throw out the old magazines you've been meaning to read or clip and save only the articles you want. Feeling lighter already?

◎ Time to tackle the clothes closet. Say good-bye to the items you've outgrown, mistakes you've never worn, and the decade-old outfits that will never come back in style. That's one less wardrobe box to move!

◎ Do the same thing with your children's clothing, toys, and shoes. Set aside anything that doesn't fit, is worn out, won't be a hand-me-down, and you don't want as a keepsake. Talk to the owner of the item before you get rid of anything. If it won't be missed, put it into your SELL, GIVE AWAY, OR DISCARD pile. If they're having a hard time with the move, you might want to wait until you're settled into your new home.

◎ Venture out to the garage. Here you have the obsolete computer equipment collecting dust on the shelf, the college textbooks, the exercise bicycle that hasn't been used in years. Time to say good-bye.

◎ Get rid of anything else that's not fixable, not wear-able, out of date, no longer your style, or is just taking up room.

◎ Casting off the belongings that you no longer need can be tremendously freeing, especially when you're making a fresh start in a new home!

Make a Floor Plan

Don't wait until move-in day to figure out what goes where and if it will all fit. On a pre-move trip, pull out your tape measure and get to work on a floor plan. This is also the time to think about any clean-up and repairs needed in your new home. If you can't get into your new residence to do this, try to obtain a printed floor plan.

In your new home, measure doors, hallways, room

sizes, window locations, and closets, as well as electrical, telephone, television, and cable outlets. Draw up a to-scale floor plan that reflects all of these details. Also take note of features that will have impact on your move. Will a stair landing pose an obstacle for your larger furniture pieces? Will you have to arrange for a hoist to move a king-sized bed in through the upstairs window?

Now measure your current furniture. Cut out paper replicas and experiment with different layouts on your floor plan. It's much easier to rearrange furniture on paper than it is to move the real pieces around the room! (You can also purchase templates in remodeling magazines and stores.) Does the entertainment center look good on that side of the room and are there enough electric outlets to support it? Will your oversized couch fit through the door of your new living room?

Check your sofas, easy chairs, and dining tables to see if their legs can be removed to fit through narrow doors, halls, or stairways. Decide whether you want to disassemble shelving units and reassemble them in your new home.

After you have determined the placement of all of your furniture, draw up a final floor plan for every room. When your movers arrive at your new home, have a copy of each room's floor plan posted at its entrance so they know exactly where to put things.

Packing Boxes

If you're on a budget, you can collect cartons at grocery, convenience, and liquor stores. Be sure to notify the store manager well in advance so they will save appropriate boxes for you. Make sure the boxes are clean and sturdy enough to hold your goods without collapsing. Secure the bottom flaps with plastic moving tape.

Packing supply stores sell boxes of all sizes and shapes, including those specifically designed for special uses. Even if you get most of your boxes secondhand, you may want to invest in a few of these made-to-fit cartons for breakable or delicate items, such as full-length mirrors, stemware, and dishes.

Use the original boxes from your electronics equipment if you still have them. If not, buy or borrow sturdy boxes as close as possible in size. Pack one piece of equipment per box.

Before loading cartons, you'll need to wrap many items to protect them from getting scratched or broken. Use clean, unprinted newspaper that you get at a packing supply or box store (it's not expensive). Never use printed newspaper; it can stain items. However, you can use printed newspaper to line the bottom of boxes holding items that are already wrapped.

To wrap items, place a small stack of paper on a flat table or countertop. Roll round glasses and jars in two or three sheets of newsprint. Begin from a corner of the sheet and fold the sides in as you roll.

Place larger or odd-shaped items in the center of the sheet and bring the corners together. Flip the item over and wrap it again from the other side if necessary. Better to use a little more paper than to lose a favorite object. When the corners are brought together, secure them with tape.

Before packing the cartons, line the bottoms with a few inches of wadded newsprint for padding. Place large heavy items on the bottom and work up to lighter, more fragile items on the top. Plates, books, and records should be loaded vertically. To prevent small items from being lost or mistakenly thrown out with the packing paper, wrap miniature knickknacks and other small items in brightly colored tissue paper before placing them in the box.

Fill in any empty spaces and top the cartons off with more wadded paper, bubble wrap, or Styrofoam peanuts. Gently rock the box. If it rattles, chances are it is not properly packed. Once it is secure, tape carton flaps with plastic wrapping tape. Do not use masking tape or narrow cellophane tape.

Do not overpack or underpack boxes. If you don't put enough in the boxes, the contents can get crushed when the boxes are stacked. If you overpack the boxes, they won't close right. Keep cartons to a maximum of 50 pounds each, if possible. Pack books and other heavy items in small boxes to keep the weight down. Remember, you or someone else is going to have to lift them!

Labeling Boxes

Label boxes on the sides. If you label the boxes on top, once they are stacked you won't be able to read the label. If the contents are fragile, write FRAGILE on all four sides.

Use a number system whether you work with a professional mover or do your own moving. Assign each box a number and record it on an inventory sheet with its contents and the room it belongs in. Record all of this information on the side of the box as well. For example, you might label a box KITCHEN: POTS AND PANS or LINEN CLOSET: TOWELS so you can find what you want quickly and keep track of items. If you're ambitious or just cautious, you can also maintain an extended inventory sheet detailing everything packed in each box. Think twice before using the word *miscellaneous* on a label; it's not very helpful.

When working with several helpers or if you are moving into a very large house, you can help speed the unloading process by using a color-coding system. Along with the label, put a colored dot on each box to indicate which room it belongs in—a different color for each room. Then post a floor plan in the new house with a key to the color codes.

PACKING SUPPLIES

Boxes

Unprinted newspaper

Bubble wrap

Styrofoam peanuts

Tissue paper

Two- to three-inch-wide
   plastic tape

Tape gun

Razor blade knife

Scissors

Felt-tip markers

Tape measure

Color-coded labels

Large trash bags

Sandwich-size plastic bags

Twist ties

Glass picture and corner
   protectors

Dolly

Rope or cord

PACKING SUPPLIES FOR KIDS

Trash bags

Prelabeled boxes for
   out-of-season clothing
   sports equipment
   clothing, items for
      right after the move
   last-minute packing
   things for the road

Small boxes or bags for
   knickknacks

Unprinted newspaper

Washable markers

Plastic tape

Labels and colored stickers

Twist ties

HOW MUCH DO YOU NEED?

When moving the contents of a three-bedroom house with five to six rooms, you will need approximately:

Four dozen furniture pads
One hand truck
Twenty small boxes
Twelve medium boxes
Eight large boxes
Three dish-pack boxes
Six wardrobe boxes

One box bubble wrap
Four rolls tape
Two rolls rope
One padlock for the truck
Sofa and chair covers
Mattress covers or boxes

TYPES OF BOXES AVAILABLE

These are the types of cartons that professional packers use. You can buy them through your mover or truck rental agency or at packing supply and box stores.

Bicycle box
Crystal and glassware kit
Dish-pack box
Extra-strength box (for electronics equipment)
Extra-large box (pillows, blankets, large lampshades)
File box
Lamp box
Large box (linens, towels, and toys)

Mattress box
Medium box (pots, pans, toys, and small appliances)
Mirror box
Office moving box
Small box (books and records)
Stemware packer
Wardrobe boxes

Packing Room by Room

When packing, try to work one area of a room at a time. It's best not to mix items from different rooms in one box.

Kitchen
◉ Use up refrigerated, frozen, and canned food in the

weeks before the move. Use or dispose of all perishable items before moving. Pack as little food as possible; the weight of cans and jars adds up. If your household goods will be in storage for an extended period of time, do not pack food. If you're moving a short distance, transport food carefully. Pack boxed or canned nonperishable foods in small boxes. Tape shut opened box tops. Put jars and bottles in individual plastic bags before wrapping well in newsprint. Use up or discard cleaning products and kitchen chemicals before moving.

◎ When packing dishes and glassware, use lots of wrapping paper. Place crushed newsprint at the bottom of a dish-pack carton, in the air space and at the top to cushion the items and prevent them from moving around. Wrap each dish individually and bundle four or five similar pieces together. Pack plates, platters, and saucers on their sides. Wrap each cup and glass individually and place them in the box upside down. If you're moving a long distance, consider using cellular packing sets designed for dishware and glasses. Wrap masking tape around utensils to keep them together before putting them in the boxes.

◎ Wrap pots and pans in newsprint and pack them in medium-size cartons. Wrap small appliances individually, securing their cords with twist ties and boxing them together. Do not put shredded paper in a box with appliances because it can get into the machinery. If your microwave has a glass tray, remove it and pack separately. Cookbooks go in small cartons with their spines facing up.

◎ Empty, defrost, if necessary, and clean the refrigerator and freezer forty-eight hours before they are loaded. If the fridge has an automatic ice maker or water dispenser, make sure these are drained. Leave the doors open to air the units for a full day, taking care to secure doors to prevent accidents with children. On packing day, dry the interiors thoroughly. Remove glass shelves and pack separately. Tape all movable parts. To prevent odors and mildew on a long-distance move, put unused coffee grounds in a clean sock, tie off the sock, and put it in the refrigerator.

◉   Clean the oven, range, and dishwasher. If you're taking the stove with you, remove all movable parts, such as burner knobs, and pack separately. Tape the oven door shut. Clean the inside of the dishwasher and lock the door before moving.

◉   After your appliances are delivered to your new home, do not use them for twenty-four hours. This allows them to adjust to room temperature and avoid dam age.

◉   Pack your telephones in a box labeled LOAD LAST, UN-LOAD FIRST. Include the telephone directories from your old community.

Living and Family Rooms

◉   Professional packers cover upholstered furniture with extra-wide plastic stretch wrap to protect it from dirt, snags, and stains. You can buy it in quantity at a whole-sale discount club or purchase plastic sofa covers from a packing supply store. You can also wrap cushions in sheets, wrapping paper, or plastic bags and use them as extra padding for other large items. Sofa beds should be tied with rope or cord to keep them from opening while they are moved; keep in mind these can be extremely heavy. Break down any furniture or shelving that needs to be dismantled.

◉   Draperies can be lined with tissue paper to prevent wrinkling, placed on hangers, and loaded in wardrobe cartons. Put drapery or curtain hardware in a small plastic bag and tape securely to the rod. Will they fit the windows in your new home? If not, leave them behind.

◎ If you're moving nearby, have rugs dry cleaned while you move and then delivered to your new home. If not, send them out the week before the move and keep them rolled up and labeled for the trip after you pick them up.

◎ Lamps should be packed separately from lampshades. Remove the bulb and wrap each lamp base in paper. Cushion it carefully in a lamp box with wads of wrapping paper, old clothes, or throw pillows. Wrap each lamp shade with tissue paper to protect it from dirt or rubbing. Shades of similar sizes can then be nested in the same box. Loosely pack wadded-up paper to fill air space.

◎ Items that require professional disassembly or crating—slate pool tables, chandeliers, or large glass tabletops—should be handled by professionals. You also might want to consider having professionals build custom crates around other valuables—your eighteenth-century end table or antique Chinese porcelain vase, for example. Custom-made crates are the safest choice for antiques, collectibles, glass, and marble tabletops. Fragile collectibles that are not custom crated should be carefully wrapped and packed in dish cartons.

◎ Paintings should be protected with a covering, like glass, which should be taped to prevent shattering. Also tape picture glass before wrapping pictures in paper. Most pictures can be packed in telescoping mirror cartons or wrapped in blankets secured with twine or cord. Small framed pictures can be packed together in the same box, but they should be individually wrapped and

placed side by side in the box, not stacked. Mark them
FRAGILE.

- Weight-driven or windup clocks, such as grandfather
  clocks, need to have weights, pendulum, and chimes
  removed. You must also secure weight chains at the
  clock base with wire. Unless you know how to do this,
  have a service person prepare the clock for the move.

- If you are transporting an air-conditioning unit, check
  your user's manual for any special packing instruction
  or contact your appliance dealer.

Entertainment Room

- Disconnect televisions, stereo components, videocas-
  sette recorders, and other electronic equipment twenty-
  four hours before packing and loading. Moving them at
  room temperature prevents damage to the components.
  (Wait a day to turn them on at the other end too,
  especially in hot or cold weather.) Before disconnecting
  your home entertainment system, you may want to tape
  labels on the wires with directions that make it easier to
  reassemble the system later.

- If possible, pack electronics equipment in the original
  cartons. If you no longer have the cartons and packing
  materials, you can buy similar items at a moving supply
  store. Pack each item in its own box.

- When moving a compact disc player, check the
  owner's manual for instructions on securing the laser.
  When moving a stereo, fasten the tone arm, remove the
  needle, tighten turntable screws, and secure the dust
  cover.

- Wrap each component in a clean plastic garbage bag
  to protect it from dust and dirt, then pad the box with

bubble wrap, Styrofoam peanuts, or wadded newsprint. Securely seal the carton and mark the outside of the box to indicate that the item inside is EXTREMELY FRAGILE.

◉ Pack records and compact discs vertically, in small cartons to keep the weight down. Separate albums with corrugated paper or cardboard dividers to cushion them. Heat can damage compact discs, tapes, and records, so don't move them in a vehicle that could get too hot.

◉ Pianos are best moved by professionals. If you are moving it yourself, tie down the top and the keyboard cover. Pianos are heavy, so have plenty of helpers and use a hand truck or dolly.

Dining Room

◉ Consider letting professionals pack your china and crystal. If you pack them yourself, take great care with these fragile items. Use double-wall cartons if you can. Secure the boxes with extra tape since they will be heavy. Line the bottom of each dish carton with three to four inches of wadded paper. Carefully wrap each item in newsprint.

◉ Begin by loading plates, followed by serving dishes, and then cups. Use extra wrapping paper around large serving dishes. Cellular dividers are recommended for glasses and especially for your stemware. Top off each carton with another layer of wadded paper. Place any cracked, nicked, or scratched pieces in a special box labeled EXTREMELY FRAGILE.

◉ Silverware should be wrapped in tissue paper or in sterling cloth bags. Nest several pieces in a bundle and load them in the dish carton or small box.

◉ Detach the dining room table legs if possible. Place the hardware in a sealed plastic bag and tape the bag

securely to the underside of the table. Wrap each piece
of furniture carefully in moving blankets. Do not apply
heavy polish to the furniture before moving, as this will
encourage the blankets to slip off.

Bedrooms

◎ Leave clothing in drawers, as long as the contents are
not too heavy. If you are moving a short distance, you
can leave your clothes on their hangers and cover them
with large trash bags. Fragile items left in drawers
should be individually wrapped. Remove valuables, such
as jewelry, from drawers and do not pack them to go in
your shipment. You should either transport them yourself or send them via registered mail. Dresser top
decorations can be wrapped and placed inside the drawers or packed in small cartons. Detach mirrors from
dressers.

◎ Clothing in closets can remain on hangers and be
loaded in wardrobe cartons to arrive unwrinkled and
clean. (Some moving companies will lend you wardrobe
cartons at no charge.) Pack shoes in the bottom of wardrobes or in a medium-size carton.

◎ If you have a water bed, rent or buy a water pump to
drain it. When you arrive at your destination, it will
take a day or so for the water bed to reach a comfortable
temperature.

◎ If you are moving a trundle bed, tie the bed closed so
it will not open while being moved or loaded on the
van.

On the day of the move, remove all linens from the
beds. Cover mattresses and box springs with plastic covers or mattress boxes to keep them clean and reduce the
chance of tearing. Disassemble bed frames and tie the

rails and crosspieces together with cord. Tape assembly directions to the frame for easy setup. Nuts, bolts, and screws should be removed, placed in a sealed plastic bag, and taped to the frame.

◉ Pack the linens, blankets, and pillows from the beds in boxes, mark which bedroom they came from on the box, and label them LOAD LAST, UNLOAD FIRST. When your belongings arrive at your new home, you can make up the beds right away. This is helpful for children who are feeling disoriented and anyone who is in need of a nap. And you won't be searching through boxes at bedtime.

◉ Before packing day, talk with your children about which of their belongings they will be responsible for packing. Young children can pack their favorite toys. This helps them feel involved in the move and gives them some control over the process.

Bathrooms and Linen Closet

◉ Toss out any toiletries that will not travel well or are almost empty. Tape shut and wrap bottles in plastic bags to prevent leakage. If movers are transporting your belongings, you will need to dispose of aerosol cans, such as hair spray or deodorant, or take them with you in the car.

◉ Pack a travel kit with toiletries you will need on your trip (see Adult Travel Kit checklist on page 111). Pack another box with items you will need right away, such as toilet paper, hand towels, washcloths, soap, and shampoo. Label this box LOAD LAST, UNLOAD FIRST. Towels, curtains, bath mats should be clean and dry before being packed in large cartons.

◉   Pack full-length glass mirrors in large mirror cartons
    or wrap in blankets and tie them up with cord or twine.
    Stand them on their sides in the truck. If they are espe-
    cially heavy, crating is recommended.

◉   Bedding from your linen closet can be used to cush-
    ion other items you are packing and fill up blank spaces
    in other boxes. Or it can be packed without wrapping in
    large or extra-large cartons. Pack curtains and place cur-
    tain hardware in a plastic bag taped to the rod.

Home Office

◉   Before packing your home computer, back up all the
    files on floppy disks. Do not pack these backup disks in
    the moving van; transport them yourself in the box with
    your important documents. Check your user's manual
    for instructions on how to "park" the hard disk and
    floppy disk drive on the computer. Disconnect the wires
    attached to movable hardware, such as the modem, the
    mouse, and the keyboard. Pack the monitor, printer, fax
    machine, and other hardware in their original packing
    containers or wrap them carefully, pack them in appro-
    priately sized boxes, and cushion them carefully, as with
    your other home electronics equipment.

◉   Secure the drawers of small file cabinets with locks or
    heavy tape. Empty the contents of heavy file cabinets
    into special file folders or small-size boxes. Place books
    in an upright position to avoid damage to the spines.
    Their weight adds up, so use small boxes to prevent
    damage to your own spine!

◉   Wrap desk accessories, such as tape dispensers and
    staplers, in wrapping paper and place in small boxes.
    Nonbreakable supplies, desk trays, and other items can

be packed in medium-size boxes. Toss out old papers, files, and magazines as you pack.

Garage, Laundry, and Yard

◎   Never transport flammable or explosive fluids, such as propane, gasoline, or paint thinner, in an enclosed van. Pesticides, fertilizers, oil, gas, and caustic cleaners also cannot be shipped.

◎   Drain the lawn mower and other power tools of hazardous fluids. Burn out any of the remaining propane in your gas barbecue tank. Clean the grease off the barbecue grill and put removable parts in plastic bags inside the unit. Call your city sanitation department to find out how to dispose of hazardous wastes.

◎   Disconnect and drain washing machine hoses. Place a plastic bag over the end of the hose and secure it with a rubber band to prevent leaks. Motors should be secured with a special tub insert that wedges between the tub and walls.

◎   Small hand tools, children's toys, and sports equipment can be packed in small or medium-size cartons. Shovels, rakes, and brooms should be bundled in a furniture pad.

◎   Wash and dry the inside of garbage containers you plan to take with you. Drain and coil yard hoses.

◎   Bicycles can be transported in bicycle boxes or loaded as is. You may want to remove the pedals. Wipe off excessive grease or dirt.

Cars and Boats

◎   If you are moving an automobile or truck in your moving van, drain the gas tank and check for any oil, battery acid, or radiator fluid leaks that might damage the other contents of your shipment. If you're moving a boat, drain all fuel or oil from its motor. Remember to give your vehicle's keys to the driver.

Time Out

When you can't face one more closet's worth of clutter or another box, it's time to take a few hours off. Here are some suggestions for a miniescape:

- Make a cup of hot tea and call a good friend for some moral support.
- Pamper yourself with a therapeutic massage, facial, or sauna at a local spa or beauty salon.
- Take a bike ride, go for a swim, play a game of tennis, work out at the gym. Exercise can be invigorating, even when you feel physically spent.
- Pick up your pruning shears and trowel and lose yourself in the garden. Arrange a beautiful bouquet for your dining room table.
- Pack up the kids for an afternoon at the local zoo or children's museum. Order take-out food for dinner when you get home and eat off paper plates.
- Escape to a matinee or have lunch in your favorite cafe.

ADULT TRAVEL KIT

Comfortable clothing	Credit cards
Toiletries and cosmetics	Sunglasses
Toothbrushes	Glasses or contact lenses
Tissues	Pillow and blankets

Camera, film

Moving documents and
phone numbers

Address book

Bottled water

Paper towels

Premoistened towelettes

Razor

Hair dryer

Travel alarm clock

Aspirin, bandages

Flashlight

Prescriptions and medicines

Important documents and
records file

House keys

Spare car keys

Itinerary, reservations,
tickets

Route map

Map of your new city

Certified or traveler's checks
for the movers

Food for the trip

KIDS' TRAVEL KIT

Baby's changing and
feeding items

Other baby equipment

Favorite doll or teddy bear

Car games

Books

Toys and cards

Pillows and favorite
blankets

Favorite music or story
tapes

Pajamas

Sweater or jacket

Clothes to last until truck
arrives

Toothbrush

Toiletries

Prescriptions, medicines

Night-light

Notebook

Pencils and crayons

Snacks

PET TRAVEL KIT

Food for several days

Water for several days

Food and water bowls

Leash

Familiar toy or blanket

New identification tag

Kennel or car carrier

All veterinarian records

CAR KIT

Tools
Aerosol tire inflator
Jack and lug wrench
Fire extinguisher
Flashlight
Road maps and compass
Driver's license

Car registration
Auto insurance cards
Duplicate keys
Litter basket
Bottled water
Ice chest
First-aid kit

REGISTERED MAIL
OR TAKE WITH YOU

Jewelry
Furs
Silverware
Stamp or coin collections
Photos, slides, home videos

Important documents and
    records
Any other items of
    extraordinary value

IMPORTANT DOCUMENTS AND RECORDS

Medical and dental records
    (with X rays)
Names of new or
    recommended doctors
Children's inoculation
    records
Prescriptions for
    medications, eyeglasses
Pet records
School and college papers,
    including transcripts,
    lists of books, and
    current subjects

Legal documents and
    titles
Home sale and purchase
    records
Household inventory
Employment records
Banking and financial
    records
Stock and bond certificates
Tax returns
Birth certificates
Passports
Insurance documents,

including household,
auto, medical, personal
Auto licensing and
registration
Driver's license
Traveler's checks
Checkbook and blank
checks

Credit cards
Moving documents,
including agent phone
numbers
Map of your new city
Address book

LAST LOADED, FIRST UNLOADED BOXES

Cleaning Supplies
Mop and broom
Vacuum cleaner
Dust cloth
Cleaning products
Sponges
Toilet scrub brush
Pail
Shelf liner
Ladder or step stool

Packing Supplies
Razor knife
Scissors
Large trash bags
Tape measure

General Household
Telephones
Lamps
Light bulbs
Extension cords
Tool kit with hammer, screwdriver, wrench, nails, screws

Flashlight
Candles and matches
Radio with batteries
Local map
Important phone numbers
Fuses

Bedroom and Bath
Sleepwear, slippers, robe
Bed linens, pillow and blankets
Alarm clock
Lamps
Toilet paper
Towels and washcloths
Soap
Toiletries
Iron

Children's Bedrooms
Pajamas, robe, slippers
Clothes for two days
Linens, blankets, pillows
Night-light
Favorite toys, stuffed animals, books, games

Kitchen
Disposable plates, cups, and utensils
Dish soap and sponges
Paper towels
Pots and pans
Basic cooking utensils
Can opener
Foil or plastic wrap
Plastic containers

Orange juice pitcher
Garbage can and bags
Coffee pot and supplies

Adult SOS Kit

At the end of the move-in day, you will appreciate having a few little luxuries on hand for a well-deserved break.

Champagne, beer, wine, sparkling water, herbal tea
Cookies, cheese and crackers, fruit
Scented candles and matches
Bubble bath, soap, shampoo
Massage oil or lotion
Comfortable clothes and nightwear
Portable radio or tape player, favorite music
Book, journal, pen
Exercise wear

Children

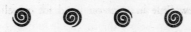

As soon as you make the decision to move, tell your children. Don't let them overhear the news by accident. Talk to them openly about all aspects of the move, especially those that affect them directly. Answer their questions with as many details as their age and maturity call for. Be positive and enthusiastic. Children will look to you for clues as to how they should respond.

Answer Their Questions

Children will typically want to know when, where, and why you are moving. They'll wonder if they will be able to see their friends again and if there are any children their age in the new neighborhood. They'll be curious about the new house, neighborhood, and school.

Explain the details of the moving process to younger children, who may not understand what it means. Reassure them that the whole family is moving together and that you are taking everything with you. Listen to the concerns of elementary-age children and point out to them all the benefits of your new home. Allow them to express feelings of sadness or worry. Be patient with teenagers, who may be upset about the prospect of leaving longtime friends. If they are entering their senior year and are concerned that a move would jeopardize their academic standing, consider letting them stay behind for the last year of high school with a relative or friend.

Take the time to sit down with each of your children on a regular basis before the move for informal talks. Listen and respond to their questions and concerns, keep them informed of the move schedule, and talk about ways to make everyone's transition to the new home smoother. Devote a section of your family bulletin board to a move calendar, notes about the move, and list of things that need to get done.

Keep Their Needs in Mind

Let children participate in the move, so they feel more in control of the process. They can help pack, accompany you on house-hunting trips, be responsible for caring for their pets during the move and design furniture layouts for their new bedrooms. If possible, take them to the new home before you move so they can get acquainted with it. They'll be very interested in finding out what their bedrooms look like.

Consider relocating at the end of the summer or during the school year so they won't have to spend the whole summer on their own. It's easier for kids to jump into things and meet other kids while attending school than in the middle of summer vacation.

If they play on a soccer team or are in a scout troop, set them up in similar activities in the new community as soon as possible.

Before moving, visit your children's current school

and get the names and descriptions of the books they are using so the new teachers can get an idea of the curriculum. Ask about any special programs each child is involved in, so you can request continuation of these programs in their new school.

Making Good-bye Easier

Here are some ways to help your children make the transition from their old home and friends to the new home.

- Show them a floor plan of your new home and discuss the house layout and bedroom assignments with them. Give each of them a small budget to decorate their new rooms.

- Give them a photo of your new home to look at and show to classmates and friends.

- Post a pre-move calendar so they know what the packing and moving schedule is. Make a pre-move checklist for them of what you both have agreed they will do to help with the move.

- Schedule good-bye visits to your children's favorite places—the local park, skating rink, or restaurant.

- Buy them small autograph books to collect personal messages, addresses, and phone numbers from friends and suggest an autograph or going-away party. Encourage your children to take the time to say good-bye to their friends and exchange phone numbers and addresses. Give them a few preaddressed postcards to pass out to their friends.

- Buy them each a disposable camera to take pictures of their friends, the house, and the neighborhood, as well as a scrapbook or photo album. Take pictures of them with their best pals.

◉ Have the older kids send change-of-address cards to magazines to which they subscribe. Make sure they have a good supply of stationery, stamps, and postcards to keep in touch with friends.

◉ If you are moving nearby, take them to the new neighborhood for exploration trips.

◉ If the home you are moving into was occupied by a family with children, ask if they will leave the names, ages, and addresses of neighborhood children, as well as their favorite play areas and popular neighborhood hangouts.

Kids' Packing Checklist

Get children involved in the move by letting them pack up some of their own belongings. Depending on their age and maturity levels, you may want to help them or oversee their efforts. Make sure they have all the packing supplies they need to do it right. Here are some things they can do.

◉ Put all broken toys, torn clothing, and old papers in a trash box. Put toys they don't want or clothes that don't fit in a separate box for a garage sale or charity donation.

◉ Return toys, books, sports equipment, clothes, video games they have borrowed. Retrieve any that they loaned out. Pay library fines.

◉ Write their name and new address on each of the packing boxes so they begin to memorize it.

◉ Pack the rest of their collections, books, stuffed animals, trophies, figurines, shoes, sports equipment, clothes, and toys in individual boxes and label them. Put out-of-season clothes and equipment in a separate box.

(Show them how to pack breakable items and what boxes they should use for each type of item.)

◉ Put their favorite clothes, teddy bear, blanket, and toys in a suitcase to take with them to the new house. Also put together a day pack with books, small toys, games, a notebook, crayons, and snacks to entertain them on the trip. Decide what they will wear on moving day.

Helping Children Adjust

Once the family gets settled in the new home, encourage your children to jump right in and get to know the new neighborhood. Don't push or pressure them to find friends, but be encouraging.

Remind them to keep an open mind when talking to kids who seem different than those they knew in the old neighborhood. Let them know it's okay to feel nervous or shy at first. Reassure them that if they keep a friendly attitude, show interest in other people, and be themselves, they will eventually make new friends that they like just as well as the old ones.

Be a good example to them by doing the same thing yourself and getting to know other adults in the neighborhood. Invite people over for barbecues and other casual events and tell them to bring their children. Some other ideas:

◉ Take the kids with you to run errands so they get to know the neighborhood. When you get a minute, help them draw up a map that shows their school, the playground, the shopping center, and the swimming pool.

◉ Go on family walks or bike rides and introduce your-
selves to new neighbors.

◉ Set up a weekly outing to a place you haven't been
yet: library, local museum, toy store, the zoo.

◉ If you move during the summer, enroll the kids in a
swim class or recreation program or local day camp so
they can meet other children right away.

◉ Buy a family membership in a local tennis, swim, or
ski club. Get the whole family involved in scouts,
church or synagogue, or a cultural organization. Encourage your teenagers to pursue their interests by be-
coming active in a theater group, a photography club, a
service group, or team sports.

◉ Encourage them to get out where they can meet new
friends. They can go skating, walk the dog, ride their
bikes, go to the basketball court, take a ballet class, join
in a crafts workshop. Invite them to bring new friends
to your home to play or have lunch.

◉ Give them another disposable camera, this time to
take pictures of their new neighborhood to send to their
old friends. This is also a great way for them to get out
and really look at their new surroundings. Remind them
to send postcards or letters whenever they miss people.

Pets

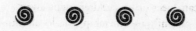

nimals also react to changes in their environment. Some pets get caught up in the excitement of a move. They will be playing in boxes and tagging along after you as you rearrange furniture. Others may show their anxiety by hiding under a bed for a few days or barking excessively. Treat them sensitively. Your pet will soon adjust.

If you're moving out of the immediate area, schedule an examination with the veterinarian. Obtain copies of your pet's health and vaccination records and update your pet's identification tags with your new address. Each state has different requirements for health certificates and entry permits for pets; check with your veterinarian.

Talk to your vet about things you can do to make your move easier on your pet. Some may suggest a tranquilizer for a long trip or an excitable pet. Ask about the side effects before you agree to it.

If your pet is traveling in a portable kennel, select one that is large enough for your pet to stand up, lie down, and move around in. Give your pet time to get comfortable with it. Buy the kennel several weeks in advance of the trip and leave it open in the house. Put the animal's favorite blanket and toy inside and let your pet go in and out at will.

Since animals get used to the local water, it's a good idea to take along a generous supply from your old home to last through the trip and the first few days in your new home. This will help keep your pet from developing an upset stomach. Stock up on pet food and supplies that may not be readily available in your new home.

You can take your pet with you in the car or book it on the same plane if you are flying. Your mover can also refer you to a pet transportation company that will handle the move if you can't do it yourself.

Car Travel

If your pet is not used to driving in the car, take it for short trips around the neighborhood before the move. Pack up everything it will need on the road, including foods, clean water, food and water bowls, a leash, toys, blankets, and medications.

Don't feed your pet for several hours prior to your trip. Give it light meals and drinks en route. Take it for short walks at rest and fuel stops. Always keep it on the leash. Cats should be kept in the carrier when you are driving. Never leave your animal in an enclosed locked car.

Goldfish can be transported in sturdy plastic bags tied off with air in the top. Feed them at their regular mealtimes and open the bag now and then to give the fish additional air. Rare fish may be difficult to move safely over long distances; contact the store where you purchased them to see if they will buy them back.

Birds can travel in their cages. Exotic pets may need certificates to cross state lines, so contact your vet.

If your trip includes an overnight stay in a motel, be sure to call ahead to find out if pets are welcome. Many of the national motel chains do accept pets, but there may be a deposit or extra charge. Register your animal with the desk clerk when you arrive and ask where you can walk a dog. Keep animals off the bed by bringing their own into the room. Don't leave the animal alone in the room.

When you arrive at your new home, put out all your pet's necessities, such as food, water, litter box, scratching post, bed, and favorite blanket or toy. When you let a cat out of its carrier, be sure all the windows and doors are closed. Allow your animal to explore and adjust at its own pace. Before letting your pet outside, inspect your new neighborhood for busy streets and other dangers.

Air Travel

If you decide to ship your pet by air, contact the airline well in advance to check regulations, find out what health exams are needed, and make reservations. Small animals may be allowed to ride in the cabins. Those with respiratory problems should travel there or in the ventilated cargo department. Others may go in unventilated cargo. Try to book a direct flight to reduce the amount of time your pet will be confined. You might want to book a weekday flight during slack periods when there's more room.

Most airlines sell or rent portable air-transport kennels. Pick it up in advance and let your animal get accustomed to the kennel well before the trip. Line it with layers of absorbent material and make sure it has a secure lock and good cross-ventilation. Mark the container LIVE ANIMAL and label it with your pet's name, your new address and phone number, the number of an alternate contact if you cannot be located, and special handling instructions. Attach the animal's leash to the outside of the kennel. You may also need to attach food and a water dish as well.

Don't give your pet any solid food the day of departure. Provide ample water in the kennel for the trip. Your pet should be in good health when traveling.

International Travel

Your moving company can give you specific details about travel requirements to your new country and the necessary vaccinations, rules, and regulations. Always make airline reservations for your pet and if you are traveling on two different airlines, check the requirements for both. Be aware that some countries require a six-month quarantine of animals. On a long flight, you may want to consider giving your pet a sedative.

Plants

On short trips of a hundred and fifty miles or less, some movers may let you transport your plants in the moving van. This is providing the plants are free of disease and the weather conditions are not extreme. But few movers will transport them long distances and those that do will not guarantee their survival. In that case you can move them yourself in your car or possibly by airplane or train.

Nevertheless, many nursery professionals recommend that you consider giving house and patio plants to your friends and neighbors as good-bye gifts. If you're moving to a different climate, outdoor plants will especially have a hard time adjusting. You can always take cuttings of indoor plants you leave behind; just keep them moist in moss and plastic bags during the move.

If you're moving out of state, be aware that some states have restrictions on the types of plants that can be transported across their borders. Contact the state's inspection board to see if the type of plants you want to move are allowed. Some states require a certificate of health from the home state's county extension agent.

Prepare your plants for a move in these ways:

- Give them extra sunlight for several weeks so they can store up the extra energy needed for an extended trip.
- Prune back overgrown leaves and branches about a month before moving. Cut back on feedings to limit growth.
- Repot plants from breakable pots into plastic containers.
- Remove insects and plant parasites or dispose of diseased plants. Avoid the use of harmful chemicals.
- Thoroughly water the plant the day before you move. Cover plants with plastic bags to hold in moisture and warmth. Place plants in a sturdy, open carton on the floor of your car, never in the trunk. To keep them from tipping over, anchor the box sturdily, stuffing wadded newspaper between plants to keep them apart.
- Water thoroughly when you replant.

Tax Considerations

If you moved to a different home because of a change in job location, you may be able to deduct some of your moving expenses. Before you move, talk to your accountant or call the Internal Revenue Service at (800) TAX-FORM (829-3676) and ask for Publication 521, the moving expenses bulletin, and Form 3903 for moving expenses.

Deductible Expenses

You can get reimbursed for transportation and storage of household goods and personal effects, including packing, crating, moving, storing, and insuring household goods. You can also claim travel and lodging expenses of moving from your old home to your new home—one trip per person. Meals are not tax-deductible.

If your employer gave you a moving allowance or reimbursed you for actual moving expenses, this amount is considered taxable income to you. However, you can offset this by deducting moving expenses. If your employer paid for any part of your move, the company must give you a statement showing a detailed breakdown of reimbursements or payments for moving expenses.

Save all receipts from your move. Use this record to keep track of what they are.

Who Is Eligible?

To take the deduction, you must meet these tests:

Distance test. Your new primary workplace must be at least fifty miles farther from your old home than was your old workplace. For example, if your old workplace was three miles from your old home, your new workplace must be at least fifty-three miles from that home. If you did not have an old workplace, your new workplace must be at least fifty miles from your old home. The distance between the two points is the most commonly traveled route.

Time test. If you are an employee, you must work full-time in the general area of your new workplace for at least thirty-nine weeks during the twelve months right after you move. The rules are tougher if you are self-employed: You must work full-time in the general area of your new workplace for at least thirty-nine weeks during the first twelve months and at least seventy-eight weeks during the twenty-four months right after you move.

Exceptions

You are not required to meet these tests if your job ends because of disability, you are transferred for your employer's benefit, you are laid off or discharged for a reason other than willful misconduct, and you are moving to a new home in the United States from outside the United States and meet the requirements for retirees or survivors.

You also do not have to meet the time test in the case of death.

Members of the armed forces do not have to meet the distance and time tests if the move is due to a permanent change of station. This means a move in connection with and within one year of retirement or other termination of active duty.

MOVING EXPENSES LOG

Moving Expenses	Date	Amount
Movers/shippers		
Packers		
Packing materials		
Truck rental		
Parking and tolls		
Insurance		
Storage		
Gas and oil		
Mileage*		
Travel Expenses		
Lodging		
Fares		
Car rental		
Parking and tolls		
Gas and oil		
Mileage*		
TOTAL		

* If you use your own car(s), you may figure the expenses by using either gas and oil *or* mileage at the rate of nine cents per mile.

Corporate Moves

@ @ @ @

ompanies often pay to move a new or transferring employee and family. Depending on the size of the company, the details may be coordinated through an office manager, the company's personnel or human resources department, or a professional relocation company.

Make sure you understand exactly what is covered under the terms of your compensation package. Details will be spelled out in either a verbal or written agreement. How much of the expenses the company assumes varies according to the employee's position within the company. Ask questions if you are not sure what is covered and keep accurate records of everything you spend. If you have special items, such as a boat, to move, find out if you will be reimbursed.

The basic relocation package typically includes the cost of a pre-move visit to locate a new home, packing and moving charges, and the individual or family's travel expenses to the new community. Companies often help an employee sell the current home and buy a new one.

Depending on the generosity of the package, the company may also offer to purchase your home if it is not sold within a certain period of time, provide you with a bridge loan, make mortgage duplication payments, pay for the commission on the sale of your house, cover trips home to conduct the transaction, and even chip in part of the cost of the new home.

Other reimbursed expenses might include:

- appliance servicing
- temporary storage and housing
- insurance coverage for goods in transit
- child care during the move
- transportation of large objects
- pet transportation
- auto licensing
- unexpired school tuition and membership dues
- housecleaning or maid service
- telephone installation
- recleaning, recutting, or replacing of carpets and drapes
- redecorating
- tuning of musical instruments
- emergency travel
- unusual moving expenses
- language lessons for overseas assignments
- home visits if transferred overseas

Even though your company will be paying for the move, you will work directly with the moving company to set it up. Contact your company representative to get the name and number of the agent you will be working with. The company will usually pay the mover directly. Incidental or discretionary expenses may be paid to you in the form of an allowance, reimbursement, or bonus.

Even if you have a choice of movers, it's a good idea to use the one your company recommends. They have an established relationship and the mover will want to do a good job to please a repeat customer.

Remember that anything the company subsidizes is considered taxable income. You will be able to deduct the basic expenses directly related to the move itself—packing, transporting your goods, and travel expenses for getting your family there. You cannot deduct meals, pre-move trips, and many other expenses that in the past were covered. One way a company may get around this is to give you additional compensation to cover the tax.

College Moves

◉ ◉ ◉ ◉

College students moving into a dorm or rented room probably won't have enough belongings to meet a moving company's minimum charge. For this reason, they will most likely want to consider a different way of transporting their goods. For local moves, transporting everything in a borrowed or rented truck is a logical choice. For longer distances, ship boxed or crated items by mail, packaging or express service, train, bus, or plane. See the chapter on Shipping Services for more details.

Overseas Moves

As you might expect, the price of a move goes up considerably when you're moving overseas. It's worthwhile to investigate the cost of buying an item there versus moving it. After you've gone through your things and discarded the obvious throwaways, consider putting some of your items in storage. Other things you may be able to leave with friends.

- If you are being moved by your employer, find out exactly how much weight and what items you can take.
- Be sure to take a good bilingual dictionary, an encyclopedia, a guidebook, detailed maps, credit cards, photo albums, and favorite possessions.
- Find out what goods are hard to find or expensive in the new country.
- Think carefully about what electrical appliances and home electronics to take with you and what to leave behind. Most countries use different electrical current, so you will need to buy transformers to alter the current, which can be expensive. Compare the costs of moving appliances and buying transformers versus selling or

storing them and buying new or used appliances there.
Bring brochures and repair manuals for everything you
take with you.

◉ Make use of a relocation agent if you have one available to you.

Getting Your Belongings There

Most people will divide their belongings into three
shipments:

◉ The majority of household goods are sent by boat to
the destination country and then by van to the new
home. This shipment will be in transit from four to
eight weeks.

◉ Items for a temporary household are shipped early or
sent by plane. This includes small quantities of clothing,
toys, children's furniture, and kitchen supplies to last
until the permanent house is set up. Shipping by air is
more expensive but much faster.

◉ Necessities, such as toiletries, clothing, and personal
items, accompany travelers on the journey.

◉ When figuring out how to get all of your goods there,
add up all the costs to get the real price of the move. For
example, if you add the cost of shipping your goods by
boat with the price of staying at a hotel until your
things arrive, it may be that the cost of shipping everything by air (and getting them sooner) is not that high
after all.

◉ Have your moving company ship your car overseas or
use an independent automobile transporter. Check all
the requirements for importing vehicles, so you don't
get surprised by import or export fees.

◎   Door-to-door replacement value coverage is highly recommended on an international move.

Choosing a Company

◎   An international moving company can handle all the travel arrangements for you, including paperwork, packing, shipping, and door-to-door delivery. Movers can arrange both sea and air shipments. They are often a plentiful source of information about the moving process and about relocating in the new country.

Choose a company experienced in overseas moves. You are paying for its experience, resources, and contacts. For example, when your shipment docks at its destination port, it will have to be shepherded through customs by an agent. Then a local mover will have to load your goods at the dock and take them to the house. Choose a company that already has these relationships set up, so that you get a good price and service.

A company representative will come to your home and give you a complete estimate based on estimated weight, square footage, and density of your goods. Depending on how much you are moving, the company will either bring a wooden or metal "lift van" container to your home to load your goods into or it will build a wooden crate to fit your shipment. The container is then loaded onto the ship.

◎   You can use a freight forwarder to move your goods by air or sea. This type of shipper will pick up your goods, box and crate them, and transport them overseas. (You will pack them yourself unless you specify otherwise.) The company may arrange to have your goods consolidated, or transported, with other shipments to

save money. You may be responsible for getting everything through customs and hiring your own mover on
the other end to pick up your goods at the dock. Because you are doing more of the work yourself with a
freight forwarder, the cost may be less than with a full-
service mover.

If you decide to use a freight forwarder, check the
company out well. Find out what kind of liability coverage it offers and who is providing it. (Think twice before using a company that is self-insured.) Be aware that
your goods may not be covered if you pack them yourself.

◎ You can ship things yourself by air cargo or air express. However, you may have to handle customs and
other paperwork yourself. You can also use the postal
service to mail boxes overseas.

Before You Go

◎ Obtain a passport and, if necessary, a visa. Obtain
necessary immunizations. Get an international driver's
license through the Automobile Association of America
(AAA).

◎ Order copies of birth and marriage certificates, school
transcripts, and other necessary documentation.

◎ Get as much information as you can about the country by contacting the consulate, embassy, tourist bureau,
chambers of commerce, libraries, travel agents. Subscribe to local newspapers, buy maps and travel books.
You'll need to get information on customs, language,
weather, transportation, local currency, and availability
of everyday items.

◎ Contact your doctor or pharmacist for the generic

name of your prescriptions so they can be filled overseas
and bring an extra supply to last until you are settled.
Obtain your medical records. Get prescriptions for
glasses and contact lenses and bring an extra pair along
with contact lens fluid. Pack a first-aid kit, including
medications for travel sickness and upset stomach. For
information on English-language medical services in
your country, contact the International Association for
Medical Assistance to Travelers at (716) 754-4883.

⊚   Meet with your attorney to bring your will up to date.
Make arrangements for what procedures to follow in the
event of an emergency, death, or illness. Get legal advice
about signing contracts or leases in your new country.

⊚   Consult with your accountant and stock broker about
tax considerations of your move, buying and selling
property abroad, handling stock, and getting your fi-
nances in order before you go.

⊚   Contact your insurance agent to see about coverage
for your household possessions in your new home.

⊚   Get a list of overseas schools for your children from
the library or other sources and write or phone the
schools for brochures and applications. Visit schools on
a pre-move trip, if possible. Get school records and test
scores before you go.

Settling into Your New Home

Congratulations! You're here! Now begins the settling-in process. It's time for getting your home organized, arranged, and decorated exactly as you want. You'll be meeting new people at home, work, and school. And you'll learn your way around your new community. Here are some typical things that you may need to do:

- Install new locks and give an extra set of keys to a friend, relative, or neighbor.
- Finish unpacking, organizing, and arranging furniture, as well as putting up art and setting up storage areas.
- Arrange to have new phone jacks installed if necessary.
- Put up window shades or blinds, draperies and curtains. Install weather stripping on windows, put up storm windows, screens.
- Complete wallpapering, carpet installation, and painting. Purchase new furniture and accessories.
- Make sure the post office knows you're moved in.

◎   Get in touch with your neighborhood welcome service.

◎   Register kids in school if they aren't yet. Find the school bus stop.

◎   Locate all the services you need:
- post office
- dry cleaner
- grocery
- bank, cash machine
- library
- park
- recreation center
- video rental
- bookstore
- movie theaters
- shopping mall
- health club, pool, courts
- good restaurants

◎   Confirm that your mail is being forwarded. Renotify the post office of your move if necessary.

◎   Order new checks, library card, driver's license.

◎   Register to vote.

◎   Take a walk or bike ride around the neighborhood regularly.

◎   Introduce yourself to neighbors and invite them over for casual get-togethers as soon as you get settled. Find out where neighborhood children live and play.

◎   Get involved in your local church or synagogue, clubs and organizations.

Important Numbers

EMERGENCY

Ambulance _____

Doctor _____

Fire department _____

Home security company _____

Hospital _____

Pharmacist _____

Poison control center _____

Police _____

UTILITIES

Cable TV _____

Electric _____

Gas _____

Oil _____

Telephone _____

Water _____

Other _____

OTHER
Accountant _____

Attorney _____

Auto repair _____

Banks _____

Church/synagogue _____

Contractors _____

Dentist _____

Electrician _____

Gardener _____

Insurance broker _____

Mortgage lender _____

Moving company _____

Painter _____

Plumber _____

Real estate agent _____

Schools _____

Other _____

Moving Calendar

Six Weeks Before the Move

	Morning	Afternoon	Evening
Monday			
Tuesday			
Wednesday			
Thursday			
Friday			
Saturday			
Sunday			

Five Weeks Before the Move

	Morning	Afternoon	Evening
Monday			
Tuesday			
Wednesday			
Thursday			
Friday			
Saturday			
Sunday			

Four Weeks Before the Move

	Morning	Afternoon	Evening
Monday			
Tuesday			
Wednesday			
Thursday			
Friday			
Saturday			
Sunday			

Three Weeks Before the Move

	Morning	Afternoon	Evening
Monday			
Tuesday			
Wednesday			
Thursday			
Friday			
Saturday			
Sunday			

Two Weeks Before the Move

	Morning	Afternoon	Evening
Monday			
Tuesday			
Wednesday			
Thursday			
Friday			
Saturday			
Sunday			

One Week Before the Move

	Morning	Afternoon	Evening
Monday			
Tuesday			
Wednesday			
Thursday			
Friday			
Saturday			
Sunday			

Week of the Move

	Morning	Afternoon	Evening
Monday			
Tuesday			
Wednesday			
Thursday			
Friday			
Saturday			
Sunday